A – Z OF RAIL REOPENINGS

A catalogue of stations and lines opened and proposed throughout Britain's rail network, with commentaries on Seeking Re-openings and New Railways around Europe.

GW00746551

Edited by Alan Bevan fc
Railway Development Sc

Printed March 1998
by Warwick Printing Company Ltd.
Theatre Street
Warwick CV34 4DR
Telephone: 01926 491666

ISBN: 0 901283 13 4

INTRODUCTION

It is very encouraging for rail promoters to record the re-opening of so many stations and lines over the last 50 years given the past climate of closures and the inexorable growth in car ownership.

Rail still has immense latent potential to provide fast, safe, attractive public transport to relieve our congested, polluted and dangerous roads.

The economic, social and environmental grounds for increasing rail development are overwhelming and urgent. Hopefully this book will help enhance the case for substantial investment in rail transport

Cover Photo: H.R.H. Prince Charles opening Newstead Station on the Robin Hood Line.
May 1993
Photo: Central Trains.

Rear Cover: Rugeley Town, Gala Opening Day, 1.6.97
Photo: Ken Russell.

DEDICATION

I am pleased to have helped finance this book in memory of my late Mother, Edith Davis, who in the 1920's worked in the salaries section of the Midland and later the London, Midland & Scottish Railway at Derby.

In this capacity she had regular correspondence with the staff at many Scottish stations, some now defunct (e.g. Dalnaspidal), some just hanging on to viability (e.g. Dalwinnie), and some still thriving. So it seemed particularly fitting to commemorate her life in this way.

Despite he increasing frailty I was still taking her, a keen rail traveller, on holidays to Scotland in her 90's, using the Anglo-Scottish sleepers which, of course, passed through, the next morning, those very stations with which she had dealt 70 years previously.

John Davis
Member of R. D. S.

CONTENTS

Chapter 1
FROM ABERCYNON ... TO YSTRAD

A grand total of 314 new and reopened British Rail/Railtrack stations are catalogued here in A – Z order. The list relates to stations which are still in use having been opened since the 1950's. Seventy per cent of the stations have opened during the last 15 years. Many of these opened under the "experimental" provisions of statutes in 1962 and 1981 and now embodied in Sec 48 of the Railways Act 1993 which enables stations to be opened on a trial basis. Only one station, Corby, has subsequently been closed due to an irregular and unreliable service.

A

ABERCYNON NORTH, Rhondda Cynon Taff
Opened 3.10.88 along with 5 other stations on the former freight only line to Aberdare. The six 2-car platforms cost £450,000.

ABERDARE, Rhondda Cynon Taff
Opened on the site of the former High Level Station on 3.10.88 after a 34 year break, this 2-car terminal platform is one of 6 along this branch funded by the then Mid Glamorgan County Council.

ADWICK, South Yorkshire
This twin platform station opened 11.10.93 on the Doncaster – Leeds line at a cost of some £1m funded by South Yorks. PTA., Doncaster Council and an E C contribution. The facility includes a covered footbridge and a large car park.

AIGBURTH, Merseyside
On the southern section of Liverpool's cross-town Northern Line Aigburth station was opened on 3.1.78 to a Hunts Cross- Southport 3rd rail electric service.

AIRBLES, North Lanarkshire
Opened 15.5.89 at a cost of £253,000 on the Hamilton Circle to serve the residential area of southern Hamilton, a Hospital and a College.

ALFRETON AND MANSFIELD PARKWAY, Derbyshire
Newly opened 7.5.73 on the Sheffield – Nottingham line to serve as a railhead for Inter-City and local passengers from the Mansfield area.

ALLENS WEST, Tees-side
Opened to the public from 4.10.71 on the Darlington – Middlesbrough line, although originally provided in 1943 to serve an adjacent factory.

ALNESS, Highland
Re-opened 7.5.73 on the Far North Line near Cromarty Firth

ANDERSTON, Glasgow
Re-opened 5.11.79 as part of the Argyle line having previously been closed on 4.11.59

ARDROSSAN TOWN, North Ayrshire
Re-opened experimentally on 19.1.87 on the Harbour Branch. The single platform cost £20,000

ARGYLE STREET, Glasgow
Newly opened on 5.11.79 as part of the Glasgow Low Level reopening and electrification. It is now one of the busiest on the system and is due to be rebuilt because the patronage threatens to exceed the safe limits of the passenger access/exits

ARLESEY, Bedfordshire
Between Hitchin and Biggleswade on the E.C.M.L. this £630, 000 station was jointly funded by the County, District and Parish Councils. It opened on 1.10.88

ARMATHWAITE, Cumbria
Opened on 14.7.86 near Carlisle on the Settle route with the benefit of funding from Carlisle City, Eden D.C. and Cumbria C.C.

ASHCHURCH, Gloucestershire
This £1m station serves nearby Tewkesbury as well as Ashchurch village and rural communities. It was opened on 1st June 1997 with twin 97 metre platforms for some 12 trains a day each way on the Cheltenham – Worcester line. A car park and bus link has been provided. The new station was jointly funded by Gloucestershire C.C., Tewkesbury B.C., and adjacent Town and Parish Councils.

ASHFIELD, Glasgow
Opened on 3.12.93, funded by Strathclyde Regional Council, as part of the Glasgow Queen Street to Maryhill Northern Suburban Line.

AUCHINLECK, East Ayrshire
Re-opened by Scotrail on 12.5.84 at a cost of £218,000. The station had previously closed on 6.12.65

B

BAGLAN, Neath Port Talbot
This latecomer to the Swanline opened on 3.6.96. The station is located west of Port Talbot and has twin 106 yard long platforms with shelters and was provided at a cost of £650,000.

BAILDON, West Yorkshire
Reopened 5.1.73 on the Ilkley line with funds provided by Bradford City Council.

BAILLIESTON, North Lanark
Opened 4.10.93 for the restoration of passenger services on the Glasgow Central – Whifflet line.

BALMOSSIE, Dundee
Opened on 18.6.62 on the Dundee to Aberdeen line 5 miles east of Dundee. After bus deregulation it suffered from fierce fare and frequency competition at a time of rail rolling stock shortages and was reduced to a minimum service from 20.1.92

BARGEDDIE, North Lanark.
Opened 4.10.93 for the restoration of passenger trains on the Glasgow Central – Whifflet line.

BARROW ON SOAR, Leicestershire.
This twin platform station on the Midland Main Line was opened on 27.5.94 by Transport Minister, Roger Freeman, to inaugurate the Ivanhoe line phase 1 services between Loughborough and Leicester.

BASILDON, Essex.
This new, twin platform, station was provided at the Town Centre to serve the New Town and was opened on 25.11.74 on the Fenchurch Street – Southend line.

BATHGATE, West Lothian.
This very successful reopening on 24.3.86 is a terminus on the previously freight only line from Edinburgh. It is a single platform station adjacent to the town centre and, along with two neighbouring stations, cost £282,000; track and signalling improvements cost £380,000 and three new Sprinter trains cost £906,000. The costs were shared between Lothian Regional Council, West Lothian District Council, Scottish Development Agency, Livingston Development Corporation and the European Regional Development Fund. 264,000 passenger journeys per annum were predicted but by 1989 annual usage had exceeded one million

BEDFORD ST. JOHNS, Bedfordshire.
A new single platform opened on 14.5.84 for through services between Bletchley and Bedford main line. Bedfordshire C.C. contributed £40,000

B (Continued)

BEDWORTH, Warwickshire.
Bedworth lost its former station on 18.1.65 and following the diversion of the Trent Valley locals during 1987 Warwickshire funded £50,000 of the £80,000 cost to re-open this station. It opened experimentally on 14th May 1988 to a new Coventry – Nuneaton- Leicester service.

BENTLEY, South Yorkshire
Opened on 27.4.92 this £500,000 station was funded by South Yorkshire P.T.A. and is served by an hourly Doncaster – Leeds e.m..u. service.

BERRY BROW, West Yorkshire
Sponsored by West Yorkshire P.T.E. a new Berry Brow station opened on 9.10.89 on the Huddersfield – Denby Dale – Barnsley line.

BICESTER TOWN, Oxfordshire
The singled Oxford – Bicester line was re-opened to passenger trains serving a restored station at Bicester Town on 9.5.87 with funding from Oxfordshire, Oxford City, Cherwell District and Bicester Town Councils.

BIRCHWOOD, Cheshire.
A new station on the Manchester – Liverpool line opened here on 6.10.80 with twin platforms of 684 foot length, ample station buildings, covered footbridge and car park,etc., at a cost of £445,000 which was met by B.R. (£225,000); Warrington New Town (£160,000) and Cheshire County Council (£60,000).

BIRMINGHAM INTERNATIONAL, West Midlands.
This new station cost £5.9m and opened on 26.1.76. designed specifically to serve the National Exhibition Centre and the relocated Birmingham Airport terminal. The station has five 1,000 foot platforms and the vast car parking area attracts users from far and wide.

BLACKPOOL PLEASURE BEACH, Lancashire.
Opened experimentally on 13.4.87 at a cost of £58,000 met by Blackpool Pleasure Beach Company (£31,000); British Rail (£15,000); Lancashire C.C. (£10,000) and Blackpool Borough Council (£2,000)

BLOXWICH, West Midlands.
On a new site north of that closed in January 1965 this station opened 17.4.89 for Walsall – Hednesford trains on this former freight line.

BLOXWICH NORTH, West Midlands
On the re-opened Walsall – Hednesford line the twin woodframe platforms are located next to Broad Lane bridge and opened experimentally at a cost of £280,000 on 2.10.90.

B (Continued)

BRAMLEY, West Yorkshire.
Opened 12.9.83 with wooden frame platforms built at a cost of £125,000 met by the West Yorkshire P.T.E. The former station here closed in July 1966.

BRANCHTON, Inverclyde.
This new platform opened on the Port Glasgow-Wemyss Bay line on 5.6.67

BRIDGE OF ALLAN, Stirling
Opened experimentally on 13.5.85 between Stirling and Dunblane at a cost of £180,000 of which the Central Regional Council met £120,000 and Scotrail the remainder.

BRINNINGTON, Greater Manchester.
The £240,000 new station on the Piccadilly – New Mills line was funded by Greater Manchester P.T.E. and opened on 12.12.77 with two 6 car length platforms.

BRISTOL PARKWAY, Bristol.
On 1.5.72 this Inter City interchange and motorists parkway station opened following the provision of nearby Motorways. It lies at the intersection of two main railway lines to the north of Bristol and attracts 750,000 users annually.

BRITISH STEEL REDCAR, Tees-side.
Opened as new on 19.6.78 on the Middlesbrough – Saltburn line.

BRITON FERRY, Neath – Port Talbot.
Located between Neath and Port Talbot the twin 108 metre platforms with ramp access opened on 1.6.94 for the Swanline services linking Swansea and Cardiff.

BROMBOROUGH RAKE, Merseyside.
On the newly electrified Hooton line into the Wirral this new station opened on 30.9.85 and cost £200,000 which was met by Merseyside P.T.E. with a Euro grant.

BRUNSWICK, Merseyside.
Located south of Liverpool Central station on the "Northern" line this £3m station opened on 9.3.1998 with contributions from Merseyside Development Corporation and Urban Regeneration Grants

BULWELL, Nottinghamshire.
This station was built subsequent to the commencement of phase 1 services on the Robin Hood line and was opened on 27.5.94. The cost of £900,000 was funded by Nottingham City Council

BURLEY PARK, West Yorkshire.
Opened on 29.11.88 on the line from Leeds to Harrogate

BURNLEY MANCHESTER ROAD, Lancashire.
The station was opened experimentally on 29.9.86 to serve the "Copy Pit" line. The cost of £139,000 was largely met by £127,000 from the County Council.

BUTLERS LANE, West Midlands.
Coinciding with the introduction of the "new" d.m.u.'s this station was opened on 30.9.57 to serve the extensive suburbs north of Sutton Coldfield.

C

CAM & DURSLEY, Gloucestershire.
Located between Gloucester and Yate this new twin platform station was opened on 29.5.94 at a cost of £500,000 funded by Gloucestershire C.C. with contributions from other local Councils. A ramp footbridge, car park and bus link have been provided.

CAMELON, Falkirk.
Opened on 27.9.94 on the Falkirk – Glasgow and Edinburgh – Stirling routes at a cost of £1.1 million funded by Central Regional Council. It was Scotrail's 50th new station in ten years and doing very well right from the start.

CANNOCK, Staffordshire.
Reinstatement of platforms from 8.4.89 provided one of the five new stations funded by Staffordshire C.C. and West Midlands P.T.A. on the Walsall – Hednesford line.

CARMYLE, Glasgow.
Re-opened on 4.10.93 with Strathclyde Regional Council funding as part of the re-opening to passengers of the previously freight only Glasgow to Whifflet route.

CATHAYS, Cardiff.
This £83,000 station was opened on 3.10.83 to serve the office and University area of North Cardiff. The twin platforms are of pre-cast concrete and the cost was met by £80,000 from South Glamorgan C.C. and £3,000 from Mid Glamorgan C.C. When opened 600 passenger journeys per day were expected but the 5 year target was reached within the first three months! Traffic has risen by over 20% since then.

CHAFFORD HUNDRED, Essex.
With 12 car length twin platforms this station opened on 30.5.95 to serve housing and a shopping centre alongside the Upminster – Grays line.

C (Continued)

CITY THAMESLINK, London
This station replaced the Holborn Viaduct terminus which closed on 26.1.90. It was opened on 29.5.90 as St. Pauls Thameslink and was given its present name on 6.11.91.

CLITHEROE, Lancashire
On 8.4.87 this station was opened having been renovated at a cost of £2,800 to enable monthly Summertime "Dalesrail" trains to call. The costs were contributed by Lancashire C.C., the Countryside Commission, Ribble Valley D.C., and Clitheroe Town Council. From 19.5.90 the platform was used for Saturdays only service of four trains each way. From 30.5.94 regular trains also called at three other newly built stations on this line.

CONONLEY, North Yorkshire.
Re-opened 21.4.88 on the Skipton – Keighley line with contributions from the Rural Development Commission, North Yorkshire C.C., District and Parish Councils towards the £34,000 cost. By September 1989 the daily passenger journeys of 135 were double that required to justify its re-opening.

CONWAY PARK, Merseyside.
Twin 130m long platforms with escalators, lifts, emergency escape stairs and a booking hall are being provided for this £15.7m "underground" station on the New Brighton/West Kirby lines. Located north of Birkenhead town centre the station is an integral part of a 7 hectare development and is attracting contributions from the Transport Authority and City Challenge funds. It is due to open in May 1998

CONWY, Conwy.
Located within the walls of Conwy Castle the station, on the Holyhead main line, re-opened as an experiment on 27.6.87. The twin platforms of 4 car length cost £267,000 funded by Gwynedd C. C. and the Welsh Office.

CORKERHILL, Glasgow.
Costing £120,000 it was one of the six new stations funded by Strathclyde Regional Council on the freight only Paisley Canal line in South Glasgow opened experimentally on 30.7.90 to electric services

COTTINGLEY, West Yorkshire.
This new station on the Leeds – Dewsbury line opened on 25.4.88

CRESSINGTON, Merseyside.
This station opened 3.1.78 on Liverpool's Northern Line.

CRESWELL, Derbyshire
One of four new stations on the Robin Hood Line extension from Mansfield to Worksop opening in June 1998

CROOKSTON, Glasgow.
Opened 30.7.90 with the others on the Paisley Canal Line at a cost of £105,000.

CROSSFLATTS, West Yorkshire.
For £78,000 this wood framed twin platform station was newly opened on 17.5.82 to serve the Keighley line.

CURRIEHILL, Edinburgh
An experimental station re-opened on 5th October 1987 some seven miles from Edinburgh on the Glasgow via Shotts line. The £273,000 cost was met by Lothian Regional Council.

CWMBACH, Rhondda Cynon Taff.
A single two car platform re-opened here 3.10.88 on the Abercynon – Aberdare line.

CWMBRAN, Torfaen.
Opened 12.5.86 between Newport and Pontypool. The cost of £215,000 was partly met by Cwmbran Development Corporation who contributed £165,000 and also provided a 160 space car park. The station has twin 122m platforms, footbridge, waiting rooms and ticket office.

D

DALGETY BAY, Fife
Located on the Fife Circle between Inverkeithing and Aberdour this £1.8m station with twin platforms and an 83 space car park opens in March 1998 funded by contributions from a local developer and Fife Regional Council

DALMARNOCK, Glasgow.
Re-opened on 5.11.79 as part of the reinstatement of the Argyle line.

DALSTON KINGSLAND, Greater London.
Opened on 16.5.83 at a cost of £650,000 which was met by the G.L.C. and an Urban Programme Grant. The station is on the North London Line.

DANES COURT, Cardiff.
On the former freight-only "City Line" immediately west of Cardiff, Danescourt opened on 4.10.87 on an experimental basis. It is one of four stations on this five mile route funded by South Glamorgan C.C.

D (Continued)

DEIGHTON, West Yorkshire.
Just north of Huddersfield and on the site of a station closed in 1930 the new Deighton opened on 26.4.82 at a cost of £65,000 met by West Yorkshire P.T.E.

DENT, Cumbria.
Re-opened on 14.7.86 for the Dalesrail services over the Settle and Carlisle line with funding from Cumbria C.C.

DERKER, Greater Manchester.
On 30.8.85 this station opened experimentally at a location immediately north of Oldham.

DIGBY & SOWTON, Devon.
A single 108 metre long platform opened on 23.5.95 3.5 miles south of Exeter Central on the Exmouth line. The £700,000 station has an access ramp, shelter and a 500 space car park. The nearby Tesco supermarket contributed £200,000 with the balance coming from Devon C.C.

DODWORTH, South Yorkshire.
Opened on 16.5.89 on the Penistone to Barnsley line, three miles from Barnsley.

DOLGARROG, Conwy.
Re-opened on 14.6.65 on the Blaenau Ffestiniog – Conwy Valley – Llandudno line.

DRONFIELD, Derbyshire.
Midway between Chesterfield and Sheffield this station was re-opened on 5.1.81 at a cost of £90,000 funded by Derbyshire C.C. who found £60,000 and the North East Derbyshire D.C.

DRUMFROCHAR, Inverclyde.
A modest £750,000 single platform opens in May 1998 on the Glasgow-Wemyss Bay Line and is situated west of Whinhill.

DRUMGELLOCH, North Lanarkshire.
Opened as a new single platform station as the present terminus of a 1.5 mile extension from Airdrie on the Glasgow North Electric line. The station opened on 15.5.89 at a cost of £713,000 including station, track relaying and electrification but at the end of the first year started making a positive financial contribution to system costs.

DRUMRY, Dumbartonshire.
Opened on 6.4.53 on the line from Glasgow to Helensburgh.

D (Continued)

DUMBRECK, Glasgow.
Re-opened on 30.7.90 as a two platform station costing £298,000 which was funded by Strathclyde Regional Council as one of six new stations on the former freight-only Paisley Canal line actually on the site of the original Bellahouston station closed in 1954.

DUNCRAIG, Highland.
Re-opened 3.5.76 near Kyle of Lochalsh after a decision to close it had been reversed.

DUNLOP, East Ayrshire.
On the Glasgow to Kilmarnock line this station re-opened on 5.6.67 after being closed on 7.11.66. Services were increased from 12.5.84.

DUNROBIN CASTLE, Highland.
Re-opened on 30.6.85 on Summer only request stop basis on the Far North Line. It was originally a private station.

DUNSTON, Tyne and Wear.
Opened 1.10.84 on the Newcastle – Carlisle line at a cost of £90,000 shared between B.R. and Gateshead D.C.

DYCE, Aberdeen.
To serve the Airport and commuters to Aberdeen this station re-opened experimentally on 15.9.84 at a cost of £3,500 met by Grampian Regional Council. Some 75,000 passenger journeys per annum were initally expected but patronage actually reached 340,000 by 1985.

E

EASTBROOK, Vale of Glamorgan.
Opened 24.11.86 near Dinas Powys on the Barry line. It has a shelter and footbridge, serving twin platforms, and car parking provided at cost of £106,000 shared between B.R. and South Glamorgan C.C.

EAST GARFORTH, West Yorkshire.
Opened as new on the Leeds- York line on 1.5.87 at a cost of £110,000 met by West Yorkshire P.T.E. By May 1988 the expected 200 passenger journeys per day had risen to a staggering 800.

EASTHAM RAKE, Merseyside.
Built at a cost of £2m and funded by Merseyside P.T.E. this new station on the Liverpool Central – Chester line opened on 3.4.95 and is served by third rail electric trains.

E (Continued)

EUXTON BALSHAW LANE, Lancashire.
New twin platforms of 108m length have been built alongside the slow lines of the West Coast Main Line south of Leyland and Euxton Junction. The £1m station (pronounced Exton) is served by Wigan-Preston trains on a five year experimental basis and opened on 15th December 1997

EXHIBITION CENTRE, Glasgow.
This station serves the Scottish Exhibition Centre and reopened as Finnieston as part of the reinstatement of the Argyle Line but was renamed "Exhibition Centre" in May 1989.

F

FALLS OF CRUACHAN, Argyll and Bute.
Previously closed in 1965 but reopened on 20.6.88 with a £10,000 platform to serve the underground Hydro-Electric power station which has a visitor centre and tours through the access tunnels.

FALMOUTH TOWN, Cornwall
Opened on 7.12.70 to replace the terminus station of Falmouth but it proved inadequate and became an intermediate station. It was renamed The Dell when Falmouth re-opened. On 15.5.89 it was re-titled Falmouth Town. The Falmouth Station was then renamed Falmouth Docks.

FAIRWATER, Cardiff.
One of four new stations opened on the Cardiff City line and opened experimentally on 4.10.87. It was funded by South Glamorgan C.C.

FEATHERSTONE, West Yorkshire.
Opened on 11.5.92 on the former freight-only Wakefield to Pontefract line.

FERNHILL, Mid Glamorgan.
On the re-opened Aberdare branch this two car platform opened on 3.10.88

FENITON, Devon.
Near to Exeter on the Yeovil – Exeter line this station was re-opened on 3.5.71.

FILTON ABBEY WOOD, Bristol
Opened on 11.3.96 the twin 97 metre long platforms, ramp footbridge and shelters for this station cost £1.5m funded jointly by Avon C.C.,Ministry of Defence, property developers and rail companies. Located between Bristol Parkway and Temple Meads it is served by some 60 trains per day and replaces the previous Filton station.

F (Continued)

FITZWILLIAM, West Yorkshire.
Twin three-car platforms were newly opened on 1.3.82 on the Wakefield – Doncaster line. The cost of £76,000 was met by West Yorkshire P.T.E.and this included provision of a 24 space car park.

FIVE WAYS, West Midlands.
Re-opened on 8.5.78 as part of the "Cross-City" Line at a cost of approximately £300,000 met by West Midlands P T E. The former station closed in 1944 and the location is now surrounded by business, shopping and housing areas. In 1984 11,664 passengers per week joined trains at Five Ways

FLOWERY FIELD, Greater Manchester
Newly opened experimentally on 13.5.85 to serve Hyde on the Glossop line.

FRIZINGHALL, West Yorkshire.
This station near Bradford Forster Square had been closed since 1965 and was re-opened on 7.9.87 with staggered platforms on either side of a road bridge to serve Bradford-Shipley trains

G

GALTON BRIDGE (See Smethwick Galton Bridge).

GARSCADDEN, Dumbartonshire.
Situated on the Clydebank line this station opened on 7.11.60 at the time of electrification.

GARSDALE, Cumbria.
Opened on 14.7.86 for Dalesrail services with contributions from North Yorkshire C.C. for station improvements.

GARSTON, Merseyside.
East of Liverpool this station opened on 3.1.78 with Merseyside P.T.E. funds to serve the southern end of the Northern line.

GARSTON, Hertfordshire.
This Watford Junction – St. Albans Abbey line station was opened as new on 7.2.66

GARTH, Bridgend.
The original platform here was renovated and re-opened on 28.9.92 for Bridgend – Maesteg services.

G (Continued)

GATESHEAD METRO CENTRE, Tyne and Wear.
Opened experimentally under the Speller legislation on 3.8.87 on the Newcastle – Carlisle line in a partnership with Cameron Hall Developments who had provided a vast new shopping facility.

GLAN CONWY, Conwy.
This small platform on the Conway Valley line re-opened 4.5.70.

GLASGOW CENTRAL LOW LEVEL, Glasgow.
Re-opened on 5.11.79 as part of the Argyle Line re-opening and electrification.

GLENROTHES WITH THORNTON, Fife.
Funded by Fife Regional Council, Glenrothes Development Corporation and Scotrail, this station was opened on 11.5.92 after Fife Circle services had been reinstated. Glenrothes is one of the New Towns built isolated from the rail system and Thornton is the nearest practical railhead.

GOLDTHORPE, South Yorkshire.
Opened 16.5.88 on the Sheffield – Pontefract line at an estimated cost of £180,000 met partly by the South Yorkshire P.T.E. and a 50% grant from the E.E.C.

GOLF STREET, Angus.
This station was opened on 7.11.60 near Carnoustie on the Dundee – Aberdeen line at the initiative of local Rail managers. However bus deregulation and difficult train utilisation resulted in poor patronage and since 20.1.92 it is served by only one train each way per day.

GREENFAULDS, North Lanarkshire.
Opened on 15.5.89 on the Glasgow Queen St. – Cumbernauld line at a cost of £180,000 funded by Strathclyde Regional Council.

GRETNA GREEN, Dumfries and Galloway.
Re-opened on 20.9.93 on the Nith Valley, Carlisle- Dumfries, line with funding from Dumfries and Galloway Regional Council. Built as a single platform only on the site of the original station closed in 1965

GYPSY LANE, Tees-Side.
Costing £24,000 this station was newly opened on 3.5.76 on the line from Middlesbrough to Whitby.

H

HACKNEY CENTRAL, Greater London.
Promoted as a "Crosstown Link Line" station this North London Line station was newly opened on 12.5.80 at a cost of £300,000 met by the former G.L.C.

HACKNEY WICK, Greater London.
Sited further east of Hackney Central station, Hackney Wick was also newly opened on 12.5.80 for £300,000.

HADDENHAM AND THAME PARKWAY, Buckinghamshire.
A single platform station opened on 3.10.87 one mile south of the former Haddenham station closed the long gap between Bicester North and Princes Risborough. With parking for 180 cars it serves a population catchment of 25,000. The £430,000 cost had been aided by a £72,000 contribution from Oxfordshire and Buckinghamshire County Councils. Thame town is some four miles to the west in Oxfordshire. However consequent to the restoration of double track in early 1998 a new twin platform station has been constructed

HAG FOLD, Greater Manchester.
Another experimental facility opened on 11.5.87 to serve Atherton on the Wigan – Manchester Victoria line. The twin wood frame platforms cost £157,000 of Greater Manchester P.T.E. funds.

HALEWOOD, Merseyside.
The £440,000 station opened on 16.5.88 to serve a 10,000 catchment within a half mile radius astride the Liverpool – Warrington – Manchester "City-line" between Hunts Cross and Hough Green.

HALL I'TH WOOD, Greater Manchester.
Opened experimentally on 29.9.86 for £120,000 found by Greater Manchester P.T.E to serve the Bolton – Blackburn line.

HATTERSLEY, Greater Manchester.
Newly opened 8.5.78 by Greater Manchester P.T.E. to serve the Glossop line.

HAWKHEAD, Renfrewshire.
Opened on 12.4.91 as an additional station on the re-opened Paisley Canal Line it has a single platform and cost £127,000 funded by Strathclyde Regional Council.

HEATHROW CENTRAL, London.
Serving Airport terminals 1,2 & 3 a new sub-surface Heathrow Central Station is part of a £300m Heathrow Express project which includes construction of a 4 mile tunnel, new flyovers at Hayes Junction, electrification of the 16 mile route to Paddington, and a fleet of new trains.

14

H (Continued)

HEATHROW TERMINAL 4, London.
The new Paddington-Heathrow express route will terminate under Airport Terminal 4 on the south side of Heathrow and the new station is due to open in June 1998. The four trains per hour service will offer a 16 minute journey at 90 m.p.h.

HEDGE END, Hampshire.
Situated on the Eastleigh – Fareham line (newly electrified on 12.3.90) the Hedge End station near Eastleigh opened on 14.5.90. Eastleigh Borough Council contributed £350,000 to this substantial 2 platform station which enjoys a large car park area.

HEDNESFORD, Staffordshire.
The remaining southbound platform was refurbished as the terminus of an experimental hourly service from Walsall which started on 8.4.89. Operating on a marginal cost basis the service promptly achieved 50% above break-even. In May 1997 a new northbound platform opened for Rugeley trains.

HEYSHAM PORT, Lancashire.
From 11.5.87 trains began running from Manchester to connect with the Isle of Man boats at the Port station, initially titled Heysham Harbour. B.R. are meeting the operating expenses and the £60,000 costs have been contributed by Lancaster City Council, The Isle of Man Steamship Company and Lancashire County Council

HOMERTON, Greater London.
At a cost of £444,000 this new station was funded by the G.L.C. and opened on 13.5.85 in the Hackney area of the North London Line.

HONEYBOURNE, Worcestershire.
With minimal expenditure this rural single platform was re-opened on the Oxford – Worcester "Cotswolds" line on 25.5.81..

HORNBEAM PARK, North Yorkshire.
The £413,000 cost of this new 2 platform station was shared amongst Harrogate B.C., North Yorkshire C.C., Harrogate College, Hornbeam Business Park, I.C.I., Homeowners Friendly Society and Regional Railways. It opened on 24.8.92 and has an 80 space car park.

HORTON IN RIBBLESDALE, North Yorkshire.
Opened on 14.7.86 with grants from North Yorkshire C.C. and Craven D.C. following the success of the Dalesrail charter services run since 1974.

H (Continued)

HOW WOOD, Hertfordshire.
The 4 car platform opened on 22.10.88 following £81,000 funding from Herts C.C. and the local Parish Council for trains on the Watford – St Albans Abbey branch.

HUCKNALL, Nottinghamshire.
The first "Fun Day" trains called at this new platform on 8.5.93 followed by regular services from 17.5.93 which link Nottingham and Newstead in Phase 1 on the Robin Hood line scheme. A large car park is provided at the station.

HUMPHREY PARK, Greater Manchester.
This experimentally opened station cost £86,000 and is located on the Warrington – Manchester line. Services commenced on 15.10.84

HYNDLAND, Glasgow.
Opened 7.11.60 following electrification of the Airdrie to Helensburgh Line and replaces the former Hyndland terminal station.

I

I.B.M. HALT, Inverclyde.
Opened on 8.5.78 on the Wemyss Bay electrified line and jointly funded by British Rail, Strathclyde Regional Council and I.B.M.

ISLIP, Oxfordshire.
Funded by several local councils the new £72,000 platform opened on 13th May 1989 to a much increased Oxford – Bicester train service.

IVYBRIDGE, Devon.
This £1.5m station was co-funded by Devon C.C., Plymouth City Council and South Hams D.C. with contributions from the E.C. It has two 108m platforms, a ramped footbridge, a large car park and a bus turning circle. Located 11 miles east of Plymouth the station opened on 14.7.94.

J

JEWELLERY QUARTER, West Midlands.
One of three new stations built to complete reinstatement of the Snow Hill route this £2.5m station is situated at the west portal of Hockley tunnel. The twin platforms are 150 metres long and they opened to public services on 24.9.95. In 1998 an interchange with the parallel Midland Metro service is due to open.

CAM AND DURSLEY, Gloucs.   21.8.96.   Photo: Dr Clive Mowforth

CAMELON, Nr Falkirk, Scotland.   21.12.96   Photo: Ralph Barker

DIGBY & SOWTON, Devon.   31.8.95   Photo: Gerald Duddridge

EASTHAM RAKE, Wirral.   Opened 3.4.95   Photo: Merseytravel

K

KENTISH TOWN WEST, Greater London.
Opened on 5.10.81 in North London a mile from Gospel Oak station. Built with £400,00 of G.L.C funds.

KILMAURS, East Ayrshire
Re-opened on 12.5.84 just north of Kilmarnock on the Glasgow – Dumfries line at a cost of £238,000 funded by Strathclyde Regional Council.

KINGSKNOWE, Edinburgh.
This station was re-opened on 1.2.71 near Edinburgh on the Glasgow to Edinburgh via Shotts line as a result of a local campaign.

KIRKBY IN ASHFIELD, Nottinghamshire.
Opened on Sunday, 17th November 1996 for "Funday" services, this new station joined others built in 1993 and 1995 on the Robin Hood Line.

KIRKBY STEPHEN, Cumbria.
Dalesrail services also prompted the re-opening of this station on 14.7.86 with the help of funds from the Parish Council and Cumbria C.C.

KIRK SANDALL, South Yorkshire.
Situated 5 miles north east of Doncaster this station opened on 13.5.91 on the Doncaster to Hull line.

KIRKWOOD, North Lanarkshire.
Opened 4.10.93 along with four other stations on the Glasgow Central – Whifflet route.

L

LAKE, Isle of Wight.
Served by former London Underground trains this £80,000 station is near the site of an earlier halt situated between Sandown and Shanklin. It opened on 11.5.87 with a contribution of £30,000 from the Isle of Wight C.C.

LAMBHILL, Glasgow.
Opened on 3.12.93 as part of the new Glasgow to Maryhill Line service, funded by Strathclyde Regional Council and actually on the site of a former station closed in 1917.

LANDYWOOD, Staffordshire
New staggered platforms opened on 8.4.89 for the Walsall to Hednesford trains on this former freight-only route.

L (Continued)

LANGHO, Lancashire.
Re-opened 29.5.94 for new services on the Blackburn – Clitheroe line.

LANGLEY MILL, Derbyshire.
The cost of this £130,000 station was met by £78,000 from Derbyshire C.C., £26,000 from Nottinghamshire C.C., £19,000 from Amber Valley D.C. and the remainder from two Parish Councils. It opened 12.5.86 on the Sheffield – Nottingham line and has twin 92 metre long platforms and a car park.

LANGWATHBY, Cumbria.
Cumbria County Council funded the cost of re-opening this station on 14.7.86 for the Settle and Carlisle "Dalesman" trains.

LANGWITH-WHALEY THORNS, Derbyshire.
Located north of Shirebrook on the 13 mile Mansfield-Worksop line this station serves the village of Whaley Thorns as well as the more extensive Langwith area from June 1998

LAZONBY, Cumbria.
Cumbria County Council supported this re-opening on 14.7.86 following the success of the Dalesrail Charter trains which started opening on May 1974.

LELANT SALTINGS, Cornwall.
This station opened 23.5.78 with a large car park and one platform to provide a motorists' parkway to relieve summer traffic congestion in St. Ives.

LICHFIELD TRENT VALLEY HIGH LEVEL, Staffordshire.
With District Council funds the existing platforms were refurbished and opened to Cross-City trains extended from Lichfield City on 28.11.88.

LIME STREET LOW LEVEL, Merseyside.
Situated under Liverpool's Main Line terminal this new underground loop line station was opened on 30.10.77 serving trains running clockwise to and from the Wirral.

LISVANE AND THORNHILL, Cardiff.
Opened on 4.11.85 on the Rhymney Valley line at a cost of £181,000 this station replaced Cefn Onn station which closed on 27.9.86.

LIVERPOOL CENTRAL DEEP LEVEL, Merseyside
Opened 2.5.77 with one platform on the single loop line tunnel for Wirral trains.

L (Continued)

LIVINGSTON NORTH, West Lothian.
Opened experimentally on 24.3.86 as part of the Bathgate Line re-opening and jointly funded by Lothian Regional Council, West Lothian District Council, Livingston Development Corporation, Scottish Development Agency and European Regional Development Fund.

LIVINGSTON SOUTH, West Lothian.
Opened on 6.10.84 on the Glasgow to Edinburgh via Shotts Line at a cost of £293,000 to which Livingston Development Corporation contributed £195,000.

LLANFAIR P.G., Anglesey.
This station is on the Anglesey side of Britannia Bridge on the line to Holyhead and was re-opened on 7.5.73. It carries the longest station name in Britain —-Llanfairpwllgwyngyllgogerychwymdrobwillantysiliogogogoch!

LLANSAMLET, Swansea.
Also served by Swanline trains this station opened on 27.6.94 and is located between Swansea and Neath.

LLANRWST, Conwy.
Having renamed the existing station Llanrwst North a brand new Llanrwst station opened on the Conwy Valley line on 29.7.89

LOCH AWE, Argyl and Bute.
Opened 1.5.85 on the Oban line on an experimental basis.

LOCH EIL OUTWARD BOUND, Highland.
Opened experimentally 6.5.85 on the Fort William – Mallaig line.

LOCHWHINNOCH, Renfrewshire
Formerly called Lochside and closed on 4.7.55 this station was re-opened on 27.6.66 on the Glasgow to Ayr line to serve Lochwhinnoch on the closure of the loop line which ran through Lochwhinnoch and several other small towns.

LONDON FIELDS, Greater London.
Having been destroyed by fire on Friday, 13th November 1981 this station was restored and re-opened on 29.9.86. It lies just north of Liverpool Street on the Enfield line.

LONGBECK, Cleveland.
Sited between Marske and Redcar East on the Saltburn – Middlesborough line the new station at Longbeck was opened on 13.5.85 following an investment of £100,000 by the Cleveland County Council.

LONGBRIDGE, West Midlands.
Newly opened on 8.5.78 as part of the Cross-City line the station cost some £300,000 to provide twin 9-car length platforms and a covered footbridge.

LOSTOCK, Greater Manchester.
Opened 16.5.88 this station is situated west of Bolton on the Preston line.

LOSTOCK HALL, Lancashire.
At a cost of £109,820 to Lancashire C.C. this new station was opened on an experimental basis from 14.5.84 on the Preston – Blackburn line.

LUTON PARKWAY, Bedfordshire.
Costing some £12.5m and situated one mile south of Luton this 4 platform station which opens in June 1998 will offer parking for 1,000 cars, lifts & escalators to provide a major park and ride facility with easy access off the nearby M1 and an attractive transport link for some £1.5m air travellers annually. The 3 storey station will have 12 car length platforms and is being funded by Railtrack together with a £2.8m contribution from the local authority.

LYMPSTONE COMMANDO, Devon.
This station was opened on 3.5.76 to serve the Royal Marine training base on the Exeter – Exmouth line.

M

MAESTEG, Bridgend.
The 9 mile single track coal freight line benefited from a £3.3m investment by Mid-Glamorgan C.C. and the European Development Funds to provide six new stations and three Class 143 diesel trains. The new Maesteg platform was relocated at Castle Street adjacent to a supermarket, car park and bus services. It opened on 28.9.92.

MAESTEG EWENNY ROAD, Bridgend.
Opened 28.9.92 south of the town to serve local housing and industry.

MANCHESTER AIRPORT. Greater Manchester.
A 2 track island platform station opened on 17.5.93 within a modernistic terminal in keeping with the International Airport that it serves. The £27m development also encompassed a new 2.5Km electrified branch off the Styal line for train services to and from Manchester Piccadilly.

MANSFIELD, Nottinghamshire.
Serving the town centre this station opened on 20.11.95 as part of the £20m Robin Hood line Phase II.

M (Continued)

MANSFIELD WOODHOUSE, Nottinghamshire.
This station utilises a former goods warehouse which straddles the bay platform and track. It opened on 20.11.95 as a terminus for the Stage II extension of Nottingham trains.

MARTINS HERON, Berkshire.
Located between Ascot and Bracknell this £500,000 station was jointly funded by Berkshire C.C. and British Rail and was opened on 3.10.88

MARYHILL, Glasgow.
Opened on 3.12.93 as part of the Maryhill – Glasgow North Suburban diesel service funded by Strathclyde Regional Council.

MATLOCK BATH, Derbyshire.
On the single line from Ambergate to Matlock Town the intermediate Matlock Bath platform was re-opened on 27.5.72 following pressure from the local community to cater for the main tourist centre of this scenic valley.

MEADOWHALL, South Yorkshire.
This brand new 4 platform interchange station opened on 5.9.90 north of Sheffield. It serves a new shopping and leisure complex and has a 200 space car park.

MELKSHAM, Wiltshire.
This station was re-opened on an experimental basis on 13.5.85 to a new train service on the 10 mile Trowbridge – Chippenham line. The cost of £1,500 for a shelter and lighting was met by Melksham Town Council and Wiltshire C.C.

MELTON, Suffolk.
With a £2,350 funding from Suffolk County Council this station was re-opened on 3.9.84 and is situated on the Ipswich – Lowestoft line.

METHERINGHAM, Lincolnshire
Situated between Lincoln and Sleaford this station was re-opened on 6.10.75 at a cost of £7,415 met by Lincolnshire County Council for 2 platforms, shelters, lighting, fencing and a car park. In 1978 usage averaged 650 passengers per week.

MILLIKEN PARK, Renfrewshire.
Previously closed on 18.4.66 this station south of Paisley on the Glasgow to Ayr line was re-opened on 15.5.89 at a cost of £240,000 funded by Strathclyde Regional Council.

M (Continued)

MILLS HILL, Greater Manchester.
Opened experimentally on 25.3.85 to serve Middleton on the Rochdale line and has attracted over 850 passengers per day.

MILTON KEYNES CENTRAL, Buckinghamshire.
Newly opened 15.5.82 with five platforms at a cost of £3m met by B.R. and Milton Keynes Development Corporation. It has a 600 space car park.

MOORFIELDS DEEP LEVEL, Merseyside.
Opened 2.5.77 with one platform on the single loop line tunnel for Wirral trains.

MOORFIELDS LOW LEVEL, Merseyside.
A new island platform beneath the original Exchange terminus to serve the new tunnel linking the north and south suburban lines and opened 2.5.77.

MOOR STREET, West Midlands.
New Inter-City length twin platforms were opened on 28.9.97 on the new "through" lines alongside the now redundant Moor Street terminal station, Birmingham. It is sited at the east end of the Snow Hill tunnel.

MOSSPARK, Glasgow.
Re-opened on the Paisley Canal Line on 30.7.90 at a cost of £101,000 funded by Strathclyde Regional Council after having been closed on 5.1.83

MOSS SIDE, Lancashire.
A single platform on the Lytham – Kirkham line was re-opened here experimentally on 21.11.83 for £8,650 of which £7,000 came from Lancashire County Council.

MOULSECOOMB, East Sussex.
Opened as new on 15.5.80 for £244,000 funded by B.R. It has twin platforms, footbridge and station buildings which are served by Brighton – Eastbourne trains. East Sussex County Council contributed £6,500.

MOUNTAIN ASH, Rhondda Cynon Taff.
On the former freight line to Aberdare this platform opened on 3.10.88

MOUNT VERNON, Glasgow.
Opened on 4.10.93 as part of the Glasgow to Whifflet re-opening of a freight only line to passengers.

MUIR OF ORD, Highland.
Re-opened on 4.10.76 on the Inverness – Dingwall line.

M (Continued)

MUSSELBURGH, East Lothian.
Opened experimentally on 3.10.88 on the East Coast Main Line just east of Edinburgh as part of the Edinburgh to North Berwick electric service. The station cost £366,000 funded by Lothian Regional Council.

N

NARBOROUGH, Leicestershire.
After closure in March 1968 this station on the Leicester – Nuneaton line was soon re-opened on 5.1.70 at a cost of £3,250 for general restoration which was met by the former Blaby Rural District Council and Blaby Parish Council

NEEDHAM MARKET, Suffolk
On the Norwich – Ipswich line this station re-opened on 6.12.71 with funds from the former Gipping Rural District Council.

NEWBURY RACECOURSE, Berkshire.
Re-opened for regular services 16.5.88 and situated on the Reading – Newbury main line.

NEW CUMNOCK, East Ayrshire.
Re-opened on 27.5.91 on the Glasgow – Dumfries Line at a cost of £410,000 funded by Strathclyde Regional Council. The station has two platforms, shelters, a long ramped access, car park and long-line public address system.

NEW HOLLAND, Lincolnshire
This £20,000 station was funded by Humberside County Council to replace the New Holland Town station which was redundant following the cessation of ferry services consequent to the opening of the new Humber Road Bridge. The station is on the Barton – Grimsby line and opened on 24th June 1981.

NEW PUDSEY, West Yorkshire.
This B.R. funded new station opened on 6.3.67 between Bradford and Leeds. It replaced Stanningly 0.5 miles away and was an early parkway-style station.

NEWSTEAD, Nottinghamshire.
The single platform here opened on 8.5.93 as the temporary terminus for the £2.7m Phase 1 of the 10.75 mile Robin Hood line from Nottingham.

NEWTON AYCLIFFE, Durham.
A newly opened station on 1.1.78 built to serve the New Town.

N (Continued)

NINIAN PARK, Cardiff.
The reconstruction of this twin platform station which re-opened experimentally on 4.10.87 at a cost of £60,000 was funded by South Glamorgan County Council and serves the new Cardiff "City Line".

O

OKEHAMPTON, Devon.
Following purchase of the 18 mile Crediton-Okehampton branch line by the Camas Quarry Company, Devon County Council acquired and renovated the station and sponsored six return trains to and from Exeter on Summer Sundays which commenced on 25 May 1997

OUTWOOD, West Yorkshire.
Near the station that closed in 1960 the £170,000 development is on the Wakefield – Leeds line and opened on 12.7.88

OVERPOOL, Cheshire.
The twin 6-car platforms cost £263,000 funded by £193,000 from Cheshire County Council and the balance from Merseyside P.T.E. The station opened 16.8.88 on the Ellesmere – Hooton line

P

PAISLEY CANAL, Renfrewshire.
Re-opened on 30.7.90 as part of the Paisley Canal Line. The line had formerly run on to Kilmalcolm but was closed on 5.1.83. Part of the route was retained for freight use but the route had quickly been built over west of Paisley Canal Station. The station itself cost £193,000, funded by Strathclyde Regional Council and is a single line terminus served by diesel multiple units.

PEARTREE, Derbyshire.
Situated to the south of Derby this local station re-opened on 4.10.76.

PENALLY, Pembrokeshire.
This single platform station re-opened on 28.2.72 and is located just west of Tenby on the Whitland – Pembroke line.

PENCOED, Bridgend.
Located on the Cardiff – Bridgend main line this station opened on 11.5.92 with new 4-car length platforms staggered on either side of the towns' level crossing

P (Continued)

PENRHIWCEIBER, Rhondda Cynon Taff.
As one of six stations on the Abercynon – Aberdare lines this 2-car platform re-opened on 3.10.88

PINHOE, Devon.
Re-opened for a three year experiment on 16.5.83 and was the first to do so under the Speller legislation. Devon County Council incurred £5,000 on this facility which is located 3 miles east of Exeter on the Salisbury line.

PONTEFRACT TANSHELF , West Yorkshire.
One of three new stations opened 11.5.92 on the 8 mile long former freight-only route linking Wakefield and Pontefract for an overall cost of £1.1m funded by West Yorkshire P.T.A and an E.R.D.F. grant.

PONTYCLUN, Rhondda Cynon Taff.
Opened on 28.9.92 on the South Wales main line east of Bridgend.

PORTLETHEN, Aberdeenshire.
Opened experimentally 17.5.85 on the Aberdeen – Stonehaven line at a cost of £120,000 which was met by Grampian Regional Council.

POSSILPARK AND PARKHOUSE, Glasgow.
Re-opened on 3.12.93 on the Glasgow to Maryhill North Suburban Line, funded by Strathclyde Regional Council, on the site of the former station closed on 10.9.62.

PRESTWICK INTERNATIONAL, South Ayrshire.
A new station opened on 5.9.94 on the electrified Glasgow – Ayr line to serve Prestwick International airport. The station was funded by PIK Holdings (the airport operators), Enterprise Ayrshire, Kyle and Carrick District Council and Strathclyde Regional Council. The two platform station has lifts and escalators to a covered walkway giving direct access to the airport terminal building. The Airport operators, in co-operation with Scotrail and the airlines, have organised a through ticketing scheme.

PRIESTHILL AND DARNLEY, Glasgow.
Opened on 23.4.90 on the Glasgow – Kilmarnock line at a cost of £291,000 funded by Strathclyde Regional Council.

PYLE, Bridgend.
Located between Port Talbot and Bridgend this Swanline station opened on 27.6.94.

R

RAMSGREAVE AND WILPSHIRE, Lancashire.
In addition to the previously re-opened Clitheroe station three more intermediate stations opened to regular train services on 29.5.94. This new station is at the Blackburn end of the line.

RAMS LINE HALT, Derbyshire.
For use by football specials bringing fans to Derby County F.C.'s adjoining Baseball Ground this 263m £275,000 single platform alongside a through siding opened on 20.1.90 having been secured by contributions from Derbyshire County Council, the Football Trust, Derby County F.C., Government and B.R.

ROGART, Highland.
Re-opened on 6.3.61 after having been closed on 13.6.60 on the Lairg Loop section of the Far North Line.

ROTHERHAM CENTRAL, South Yorkshire.
Using a new 0.25 mile single track link (known as the Holmes Chord) trains between Sheffield and Doncaster began using the brand new Rotherham Central station from 11.5.87. The overall cost of £2.4m had been met by South Yorkshire P.T.E. with the benefit of a 50% E.R.D.F. grant and a contribution from Rotherham District Council.

ROUGHTON ROAD, Norfolk.
Just south of Cromer this £62,000 station was opened to Norwich trains on 20.5.85. British Rail met £11,000; North Norfolk D.C. paid £7,000 and the M.S.C. paid £44,000. It was the culmination of a nine year local campaign.

RUGELEY TOWN, Staffordshire.
As an extension of the reopened Hednesford line a new twin platform station opened on 1.6.97 close to Rugeley town centre and housing estates. Waiting shelters, a footbridge and an adjacent car park are included in the development for which the cost of nearly £1m has been met by Staffordshire C.C. and Cannock Chase District Council.

RUNCORN EAST, Cheshire.
From 3.10.83 this brand new station provides rail services on the Warrington – Chester line for new housing estates and provides twin platforms of 8 coach length, ticket office, waiting shelters, car parking, lighting and ramped footbridge. The £385,000 cost was met by contributions of £100,000 each from Warrington Development Corporation and Cheshire County Council and the balance covered by British Rail. A 30% grant was also received from the E.C.

R (Continued)

RUSKINGTON, Lincolnshire.
Re-opened 5.5.75 on the Lincoln – Sleaford line for just £8,523 paid for by Lincolnshire C.C. the twin platforms have shelters, lighting and a car park.

RUTHERGLEN, South Lanarkshire.
The station was relocated on 5.11.79 to be served by Argyle Line trains when local services were transferred from Glasgow Central High Level to the low level Argyle line.

RYDER BROW, Greater Manchester.
Opened 4.11.85 experimentally to serve the Reddish area and funded by the G.M.P.T.E.

S

ST MICHAELS, Merseyside.
Re-opened on 3.1. 78 along with Aigburth on the Liverpool Northern line and was well used for the Liverpool Garden Festival.

ST PAULS THAMESLINK. *See City Thameslink*

SALFORD CRESCENT, Greater Manchester,
Situated at the northern end of the new Windsor Link line this new island station opened on 11.5.87 at a cost of £660,000 met jointly by B.R. and the P.T.E.

SALTAIRE, West Yorkshire.
Using the site of a station closed in March 1965 the £139,000 station was opened on 10.4.84 funded by the West Yorkshire P.T.E. with an E.C. grant. It is situated near Shipley on the Skipton – Bradford/Leeds line.

SANDAL AND AGBRIGG, West Yorkshire.
Previously closed in 1957 this £180,000 station re-opened on 30.11.87 south of Wakefield on the Doncaster line and from May 1988 was also served by Leeds – Sheffield trains.

SANQUHAR, Dumfries and Galloway.
Re-opened on 27.6.94 on the Nith Valley (Glasgow – Dumfries – Carlisle) line at a cost of £375,000 funded by Dumfries and Galloway Enterprise Limited.

SARN, Bridgend.
Just two miles north of Bridgend on the Maesteg line this platform opened on 28.9.92.

SHERBURN IN ELMET, North Yorkshire.
After being closed for 19 years this station on the York – Pontefract line opened experimentally on 9.7.84 for six months following a grant from Selby District Council. As the usage was satisfactory the station has remained open.

SHIELDMUIR, North Lanarkshire.
Opened on 14.5.90 at a cost of £288,000 for a two platform station utilising an existing footbridge and land from former sidings and funded by Strathclyde Regional Council. Located just south of Motherwell on the electrified West Coast Main Line it is served by the hourly Lanark service. Much of the area was derelict but with a frequent bus service the initial patronage was very disappointing. Passengers are starting to increase and the surrounding area is being developed for housing, industry and services.

SHIREBROOK, Derbyshire.
Situated north of Mansfield Woodhouse this is one of 4 additional stations forming the Robin Hood Phase III extension to Worksop costing some £5m with contributions from E R D F, Capital Challenge, Single Regeneration Budget and Railtrack.

SHOTTON LOW LEVEL, Flintshire.
Situated on the North Wales coast line this station re-opened on 21.8.72 to give an interchange with the High Level platforms on the Wrexham – Liverpool line.

SILEBY, Leicestershire.
Located on the site of the original station on the Midland Main Line the twin platforms opened to passengers using Ivanhoe Line trains on 27.5.94.

SILKSTONE COMMON, South Yorkshire.
With a £60,000 funding from South Yorkshire P.T.E. this station on the Huddersfield – Denby Dale – Sheffield line opened on 26.11.84.

SINFIN CENTRAL, Derbyshire
On a 1 mile branch just south of Derby this station and Sinfin North (below) opened on 4.10.76 following expenditure by Derbyshire County Council. The catchment is exclusively confined to an industrial area thus patronage has been limited to peak hour traffic.

SINFIN NORTH, Derbyshire.
Newly opened 4.10.76 the single platform serves only peak hour trains. With no access to the stations for the general public the usage and success of the new stations has inevitably been minimal.

S (Continued)

SKEWEN, Neath – Port Talbot.
West of Neath this station opened on 27.6.94 for Swanline services.

SLAITHWAITE, West Yorkshire.
Opened on 13.12.82 in Huddersfield on the site of the station closed in October 1968 and funded by West Yorkshire P.T.E. with £120,000.

SMALLBROOK JUNCTION, Isle of Wight.
Opened on 20.7.91 on the singled "Island Line" specifically to provide cross-platform interchange with the Isle of Wight Steam Railway.

SMETHWICK GALTON BRIDGE, West Midlands.
This two level station has been built on a viaduct over a canal and alongside a steep embankment – hence the £3.9m cost to provide an interchange between the Snow Hill and New Street lines as well as serving urban housing and industry. Opened on 24.9.95 it now replaces Smethwick West

SMITHY BRIDGE, Greater Manchester.
Opened experimentally on 18.8.85 to serve Rochdale with Halifax – Manchester Victoria trains. Funded by Greater Manchester P.T.E.

SNOW HILL, West Midlands.
A completely new four platform station has been built on the site of the former main line station which had been closed since March 1972. The overall £8m scheme was funded by the West Midlands P.T.E. with the benefit of a £900,000 E.R.D.F. grants and covers the construction of the new stations at Moor Street and Snow Hill and the provision of new tracks and signalling. The stations opened for services on 5.10.87 for local trains to Stratford upon Avon and Leamington Spa. The Snow Hill to Smethwick link opened on 24.9.95.

SOUTHAMPTON PARKWAY, Hampshire.
Opened as Southampton Airport on 1.4.66 and developed 29.9.86 to serve both the adjacent Airport and as a commuter station for the nearby M.27 Motorway.

SOUTH BANK, Tees-side.
Resited in 1984 for a road scheme funded by Cleveland County Council and the Department of Transport. It is situated on the Middlesborough – Saltburn line.

SOUTHBURY, Greater London.
In conjunction with electrification on the line this station was opened on 21.11.60 on the Liverpool Street – Seven Sisters – Cheshunt line.

S (Continued)

SOUTH GYLE, Edinburgh
Opened experimentally on 1.5.85 on the Edinburgh to Fife line at a cost of £226,290 funded by Lothian Regional Council. It serves a large area of the western side of Edinburgh as a park and ride station and also benefits a rapidly developing commercial and industrial area. In its first year it handled 4,000 passengers per week and has continued to expand.

SOUTH WIGSTON, Leicestershire.
Opened as completely new on 10.5.86 on the Nuneaton – Leicester line at a cost of £135,000 to Leicestershire C.C. Usage has been 50% greater than forecast and extra services have been provided. Some five miles south of Leicester the station has staggered platforms and serves a large housing estate.

STANSTED AIRPORT, Essex.
The £44m 3.5 mile new rail link connects the Liverpool St. – Cambridge line with the airport terminal via a triangular junction and an electrified single line to an island platform opened on 19.3.91.

STEETON AND SILSDEN, West Yorkshire.
Built on the site of the former platforms this £260,000 station opened on 14.5.90 on the Keighley – Skipton – Bradford line.

STEPPS, North Lanarkshire.
Re-opened 15.5.89 on the Glasgow – Springburn – Cumbernauld line at a cost of £291,000 funded by Strathclyde Regional Council.

STEVENAGE, Hertfordshire.
Relocated as an Inter-City parkway 0.5 miles southwards to the centre of the new town and opened on 23.7.73 to Kings Cross – East Coast main line trains.

STEWARTON, East Ayrshire.
On the Glasgow to Kilmarnock line this station was re-opened on 5.6.67 having been closed on 7.11.66.

STREETHOUSE, West Yorkshire.
Opened 11.5.92 on the former freight-only Wakefield – Pontefract line.

SUGAR LOAF, Powys
Re-opened experimentally from 21.6.87 on Summer Sundays along the Central Wales line for use by ramblers. Sponsored by the Sports Council for Wales.

SUMMERSTON, Glasgow.
Opened 3.12.93, funded by Strathclyde Regional Council, on the Glasgow – Maryhill North Suburban line.

SUTTON PARKWAY, Nottinghamshire.
The twin 79 metre platforms opened to regular Robin Hood line services on 20.11.95 with a large car parking area adjacent. The £650,000 project was funded by Ashfield District Council.

SWINTON, South Yorkshire.
Opened on 14.5.90 the new 3 platform Swinton station was provided as part of a £33m scheme to rationalise tracks north of Rotherham and construct a new junction north of Swinton station.

SYSTON, Leicestershire.
Opened on 27.5.94 this single platform station is located south of Syston junction on a bi-directional slow line. Ample car parking is available nearby.

T

TAME BRIDGE PARKWAY, West Midlands.
A brand new £600,000 station which was opened on 4.6.90 at the south end of the Bescot freight yards on the New Street – Walsall line.

TEES-SIDE AIRPORT, Tees-side.
Opened 3.10.71 as new by British Rail on the Darlington – Middlesbrough line.

TELFORD CENTRAL, Shropshire.
With twin platforms of Inter-City train length, a large car park and surrounded by new highways and the nearby M54 the new Telford Central station affords a "Parkway" facility for a wide area of Shropshire. The station cost £700,000 and was funded jointly by British Rail, Telford Development Corporation and Shropshire County Council. It opened on 12. 5.86 on the Wolverhampton – Shrewsbury line.

TEMPLECOMBE, Somerset.
Having been closed in 1966 a contribution of £9,200 by Somerset C.C. enabled B.R. to re-open this station on 3.10.83 as an experiment on the Yeovil – Salisbury line. The re-opening was a result of a local campaign.

THE HAWTHORNS, West Midlands.
Opened on 2.4.95 this £1.6m station is close to West Bromwich Albion football ground. A 190 space car park has been provided. An adjacent interchange with Midland Metro will be available.

THEOBALDS GROVE, Greater London.
Opened on 21.11.60 on the Southbury line.

THURNSCOE, South Yorkshire.
This station on the Pontefract – Sheffield line opened 16.5.88 following £180,000 expenditure by South Yorkshire P.T.E. helped by a 50% grant from the E.C.

TIVERTON PARKWAY, Devon.
Next to junction 27 of the M5 with 250 car parking spaces this fine new station opened on 12.5.86 with full Inter-City length platforms and a colourful brick construction. The cost of £730,000 was principally met by B.R. with contributions of £80,000 from Devon C.C., £50,000 from Mid Devon District Council and £30,000 worth of road improvements by Devon C.C. It replaces the former Tiverton Junction station.

TONDU, Bridgend.
A platform at this former junction station on the Maesteg line was refurbished and re-opened on 28.9.92.

TURKEY STREET, Greater London.
On the Liverpool Street. – Cheshunt line this station opened 21.11.60.

TUTBURY AND HATTON, Staffordshire/Derbyshire.
On the Stoke – Uttoxeter – Derby line this £79,000 station opened on 3.4.89 on the site of a closed station with contributions from eight authorities. Tutbury village is in Staffordshire but the station and Hatton village are in Derbyshire.

TY GLAS, South Glamorgan.
On 29.4.87 this two-car length platform opened experimentally to serve housing, business and industrial areas on the Coryton branch line north of Cardiff. The cost of £78,000 was funded by South Glamorgan C.C.

U

UNIVERSITY, West Midlands.
The twin 9-car length platforms on a severe curve cost £300,000 with stairs, footbridge and ticket office and was funded by the West Midlands P.T.E. Opened on 8.5.78 on a completely new site the station almost exclusively serves the Birmingham University campus and the Queen Elizabeth Hospital complex.

UPHALL, West Lothian.
Opened experimentally on 24.3.86 as part of the Bathgate line re-opening with funding from Lothian Regional Council, West Lothian District Council, European Regional Development Fund and Livingston Development Corporation.

V

VALLEY, Anglesey.
This station is on the western tip of Anglesey nearest to Holyhead and was re-opened on 15.3.82 with the benefit of a £15,000 grant from Gwynedd County Council, Ynys Mon Borough and four Community Councils.

W

WALLYFORD, East Lothian.
Opened on 13.6.94 with funding from Lothian Regional Council, the new station is on the East Coast Main Line served by electric Edinburgh – North Berwick services.

WALSDEN, West Yorkshire.
Located on the Calder Valley and served by Halifax – Rochdale trains this new station re-opened on 10.9.90 after the expenditure of £240,000.

WATFORD STADIUM, Hertfordshire.
Opened as new on 4.12.82 specifically to serve patrons of football matches at the Watford F.C. ground. The single platform cost £200,000 and was paid for by £54,000 from the Football Trust, Watford Football Club and Watford Borough Council. The station which is on the Watford High Street – Croxley Green line is not in the public timetable and is served only by special trains.

WATLINGTON, Norfolk.
Re-opened 5.5.75 just seven years after being closed the intact station was repainted and refurbished with lighting and fencing at a cost of £700 to villagers plus a £150 contribution from Norfolk County Council. It is situated on a Kings Lynn – Ely line and was formerly named Magdalen Road.

WATTON AT STONE, Hertfordshire.
Costing some £140,000 this rebuilt station opened on 17th May 1982 after a notable campaign by local residents. During their three year campaign the villagers and wellwishers raised £4,000, the Parish Council funded £6,000, the District Council produced £9,000 and the balance was met by British Rail and Hertfordshire County Council. The station's twin platform can accommodate six car e.m.u's and the line links Stevenage and Hertford.

WAUN-GRON PARK, Cardiff.
Experimentally opened on 2.11.87 on the new Cardiff "City Line" the two staggered platforms costing £180,000 were funded by South Glamorgan County Council.

W (Continued)

WAVERTREE TECHNOLOGY PARK, Merseyside.
This £2m station is located east of Edge Hill on the Earlestown line and is due to open in October 1998.

WELHAM GREEN, Hertfordshire.
This Great Northern suburban station between Brookmans Park and Hatfield opened on 29.9.86 at a cost of £265,000 which provided twin 6-car length platforms on the slow lines with shelters, ticket office and car parking. It was funded jointly by Welwyn District Council, Hertfordshire County Council, Hatfield P.C. and British Rail.

WESTER HAILES, Lothian.
Serving a population of 12,000 alongside the Edinburgh – Shotts – Glasgow line this new station opened experimentally on 11.5.87 at a cost of £165,000 met by Lothian Regional Council. The station is adjacent to a new shopping centre and is located between Kingsknowe and Kirknewton.

WEST HAM Low Level, Greater London.
On the North London Line this station opened as new on 14.5.79 between Stratford and North Woolwich. It has twin platforms, shelters and car parking.

WEST HAM High Level, Greater London.
A new £3m station opens mid 1998 on the London, Tilbury & Southend line and offers interchange with three London Underground services and the lower level North London line station. Situated parallel to the L U L platforms the 12 car island platform will have a long waiting shelter, lifts and stairs. The new station accompanies a £75m modernisation of the L.T & S route and investment in new trains due in 1999.

WETHERALL, Cumbria.
For just £6,000 this station, just 4.5 miles east of Carlisle, was re-opened on 5.10.81 and is served by the Carlisle to Newcastle trains.

WHALLEY, Lancashire
Re-opened on 29.5.94 for new service on the Blackburn – Clitheroe line.

WHIFFLET, North Lanarkshire.
Opened on 21.12.92 in preparation for the re-opening to passengers of the Glasgow – Rutherglen – Whifflet freight-only line. The station is actually on the South to North Motherwell to Stirling Line and is close to the site of the original station closed on 10.9.62. The station is presently served by half hourly diesel trains on the Glasgow – Whifflet service, hourly electric trains on the Motherwell – Coatbridge service and hourly diesel trains on the Motherwell to Cumbernauld service.

W (Continued)

WHINHILL, Inverclyde.
Located on the Wemyss Bay – Glasgow electrified line a new single platform costing £258,000 was opened on 14.5.90.

WHISTON, Merseyside.
1st October 1990 was the opening date for this new station on the Liverpool – Earlestown – Manchester line. The two 107 metre length platforms and basic facilities cost £420,000 shared between Merseyside P.T.E. and Knowsley Borough Council and is located between Huyton and Rainhill.

WHITWELL, Derbyshire.
This is the northernmost of many new stations along the re-opened and succesful Robin Hood line from Nottingham to Worksop which was completed in June 1998.

WILDMILL, Bridgend.
Opened a little later that the other Maesteg line stations this platform came into use on the 18th November 1992.

WILLINGTON, Derbyshire
Located north of Burton on Trent this new station opened on 26.5.95 with two 80 metre long platforms costing £565,000 funded by Derbyshire County Council and South Derbyshire District Council.

WINNERSH TRIANGLE, Berkshire.
Situated on the Reading – Wokingham – Guildford line and north of the other station at Winnersh this new station opened on 12.5.86 at a cost of £375,000 with contributions of £150,000 from Berkshire County Council, £150,000 from British Rail and £75,000 from Wimpey/Slough Estates. It is located adjacent to extensive new office and housing developments and offers a large car park.

WOODSMOOR, Greater Manchester.
The twin woodframe platforms cost £300,000 and opened on 1.10.90 to trains between Davenport and Hazel Grove on the Stockport – Chinley line.

WORLE, Woodspring.
Featuring brightly coloured 4 car length platforms and a large car park this new £700,000 station opened to Weston super Mare – Bristol trains.

Y

YARM, Tees-Side.
The twin platforms of this new station on the Northallerton – Middlesbrough line cost £670,000 and opened on 20.2.96 to Trans-Pennine services. A 74 space car park is provided.

Y (Continued)

YATE, South Gloucestershire.
Twin 2-car platforms costing £130,000 opened here on 15.5.89 funded jointly by Avon County Council, Northavon District Council and British Rail to serve Bristol – Gloucester trains. During early 1992 the County Council funded a £124,000 extension of the platforms to take 4-car trains.

YNYSWEN, Rhondda Cynon Taff.
Between Treherbert and Treorchy this £50,000 station was experimentally opened by Mid-Glamorgan County Council with a single platform and shelter on 29.9.86 and is served by trains along the Rhondda Valley. The station has achieved a more than three fold increase over forecast traffic.

YSTRAD RHONDDA, Rhondda Cynon Taff.
An earlier station named Ystrad Rhondda has been renamed Ton Pentre and is the next station up the valley. The new Ystrad Rhondda opened on the 29th September 1986 and has two 91 metre platforms utilising a passing loop on the otherwise single line. It is served by the Treherbert – Cardiff trains and has increased usage fourfold to over 500 passengers per day.

FILTON ABBEY WOOD, Nr Bristol.   28.3.96   Photo: Nigel Hunt

Chapter 2

STATION OPENINGS : When and Where

New and re-opened stations on the British Rail/Railtrack network are given in date order. Experimental openings are marked (X)

6. 4.53	Drumry

30. 9.57	Butlers Lane

7.11.60	Golf Street
7.11.60	Garscadden
7.11.60	Hyndland
21.11.60	Southbury
21.11.60	Theobalds Grove
21.11.60	Turkey Street

6. 3.61	Rogart

18. 6.62	Balmossie

14. 6.65	Dolgarrog

7. 2.66	Garston, Herts
1. 4.66	Southampton Parkway
27. 6.66	Lochwinnoch.

6. 3.67	New Pudsey
5. 6.67	Branchton
5. 6.67	Dunlop
5. 6.67	Stewarton

5. 1.70	Narborough
4. 5.70	Glan Conwy
7.12.70	Falmouth Town

1. 2.71	Kingsknowe
3. 5.71	Feniton
3.10.71	Tees-Side Airport
4.10.71	Allens West
6.12.71	Needham Market
28. 2.72	Penally

1. 5.72	Bristol Parkway
25. 5.72	Matlock Bath
21. 8.72	Shotton Low Level

5. 1.73	Baildon
23. 3.73	Stevenage
7. 5.73	Alfreton & Mansfield Parkway
7. 5.73	Alness
7. 5.73	Llanfair P.G.

25.11.74	Basildon

5. 5.75	Ruskington
5. 5.75	Watlington
6.10.75	Metherington

26. 1.76	Birmingham International
3. 5.76	Duncraig
3. 5.76	Gypsy Lane
3. 5.76	Lympstone Commando
4.10.76	Peartree
4.10.76	Sinfin Central
4.10.76	Sinfin North
4.10.76	Muir of Ord

2. 5.77	Liverpool Moorfields DL
2. 5.77	Liverpool Moorfields LL
2. 5.77	Liverpool Central DL
30.10.77	Liverpool Lime St LL
12.12.77	Brinnington

1. 1.78	Newton Aycliffe
3. 1.78	Aigburth
3. 1.78	Cressington
3. 1.78	Garston, Merseyside
3. 1.78	St.Michaels

8. 5.78	Five Ways	23. 7.84 South Bank
8. 5.78	Hattersley	3. 9.84 Melton
8. 5.78	Longbridge	15. 9.84 Dyce (X)
8. 5.78	University	1.10.84 Dunston
8. 5.78	I.B.M.Halt	6.10.84 Livingston South
23. 5.78	Lelant Saltings	15.10.84 Humphrey Park(X)
19. 6.78	B.S.C.Redcar	26.11.84 SiLkstone Common

8. 5.78 Five Ways
8. 5.78 Hattersley
8. 5.78 Longbridge
8. 5.78 University
8. 5.78 I.B.M.Halt
23. 5.78 Lelant Saltings
19. 6.78 B.S.C.Redcar

14. 5.79 West Ham
5.11.79 Anderston
5.11.79 Argyle Street
5.11.79 Glasgow Central L.L.
5.11.79 Dalmarnock
5.11.79 Exhibition Centre
5.11.79 Rutherglen

12. 5.80 Hackney Central
12. 5.80 Hackney Wick
12. 5.80 Moulsecoomb
6.10.80 Birchwood

5. 1.81 Dronfield
25. 5.81 Honeybourne
24. 6.81 New Holland
5.10.81 Kentish Town West
5.10.81 Wetheral

1. 3.82 Fitzwilliam
15. 3.82 Valley
26. 4.82 Deighton
17. 5.82 Crossflatts
17. 5.82 Milton Keynes Central
17. 5.82 Watton-at-Stone
4.12.82 Watford Stadium
13.12.82 Slaithwaite

16. 5.83 Pinhoe (X)
17. 5.83 Dalston Kingsland
12. 9.83 Bramley
3.10.83 Cathays
3.10.83 Runcorn East
3.10.83 Templecombe (X)
21.11.83 Moss Side (X)

10. 4.84 Saltaire
12. 5.84 Kilmaurs
12. 5.84 Auchinleck
14. 5.84 Bedford St. Johns
14. 5.84 Lostock Hall (X)
9. 7.84 Sherburn in Elmet (X)

23. 7.84 South Bank
3. 9.84 Melton
15. 9.84 Dyce (X)
1.10.84 Dunston
6.10.84 Livingston South
15.10.84 Humphrey Park(X)
26.11.84 SiLkstone Common

23. 3.85 Mills Hill (X)
1. 5.85 Loch Awe (X)
1. 5.85 South Gyle (X)
6. 5.85 Loch Eil O.B. (X)
13. 5.85 Bridge of Allan (X)
13. 5.85 Flowery Field (X)
13. 5.85 Homerton
13. 5.85 Melksham (X)
13. 5.85 Longbeck
17. 5.85 Porthleven (X)
20. 5.85 Roughton Road
30. 6.85 Dunrobin
18. 8.85 Smithy Bridge (X)
30. 9.85 Bromborough Rake
30. 9.85 Derker(X)
4.11.85 Lisvane & Thornhill
4.11.85 Ryder Brow (X)

24. 3.86 Bathgate (X)
24. 3.86 Livingston North (X)
24. 3.86 Uphall (X)
10. 5.86 South Wigston
12. 5.86 Cwmbran
12. 5.86 Langley Mill
12. 5.86 Telford Central
12. 5.86 Tiverton Parkway
12. 5.86 Winnersh Triangle
14. 7.86 Armathwaite
14. 7.86 Dent
14. 7.86 Garsdale
14. 7.86 Horton in Ribblesdale
14. 7.86 Kirkby Stephen
14. 7.86 Langwathby
14. 7.86 Lazonby
29. 9.86 Hall i'th Wood (X)
29. 9.86 London Fields
29. 9.86 Welham Green
29. 9.86 Ynyswen
29. 9.86 Ystrad Rhondda
29. 9.86 Burnley Man' Road(X)
24.11.86 Eastbrook

19. 1.87	Ardrossan Town (X)	3. 4.89	Tutbury & Hatton
8. 4.87	Clitheroe	8. 4.89	Hednesford (X)
13. 4.87	Blackpool P.B. (X)	8. 4.89	Cannock (X)
29.4.87	Ty Glas (X)	8. 4.89	Landywood (X)
1. 5.87	East Garforth	17. 4.89	Bloxwich
9. 5.87	Bicester Town (X)	15. 5.89	Airbles
11. 5.87	Hag Fold(X)	15. 5.89	Dodsworth
11.5.87	Heysham Port(X)	15. 5.89	Greenfaulds
11. 5.87	Lake	15. 5.89	Islip
11. 5.87	Rotherham Central	15.5.89	Milliken Park
11. 5.87	Salford Crescent	15.5.89	Stepps
11. 5.87	Wester Hailes (X)	15. 5.89	Yate
21. 6.87	Sugar Loaf(X)	16. 5.89	Drumgelloch
27. 6.87	Conwy (X)	29. 7.89	Llanrwst
3. 8.87	Gateshead Metro Centre (X)	9.10.89	Berry Brow
7. 9.87	Frizinghall	20. 1.90	Rams Line Halt
28.9.87	Moor Street	23.4.90	Priesthill & Darnley
3.10.87	Haddenham&ThameParkway	14. 5.90	Whinhill
4.10.87	Danes Court (X)	14. 5.90	Hedge End
4.10.87	Fairwater (X)	14. 5.90	Steeton & Silsden
4.10.87	Ninian Park (X)	14. 5.90	Shieldmuir
5.10.87	Curriehill (X)	14. 5.90	Swinton
5.10.87	Snow Hill	29. 5.90	City Thameslink
2.11.87	Waun-Gron Park(X)	4. 6.90	Tame Bridge
30.11.87	Sandal & Agbrigg	30. 7.90	Corkerhill (X)
		30. 7.90	Crookston (X)
		30. 7.90	Dumbreck (X)
21. 4.88	Cononley	30.7.90	Mosspark (X)
25. 4.88	Cottingley	30. 7.90	Paisley Canal (X)
14. 5.88	Bedwortb (X)	5. 9.90	Meadowhall
16. 5.88	Goldthorpe	10. 9.90	Walsden
16. 5.88	Halewood	24. 9.90	Worle
16. 5.88	Lostock	1.10.90	Whiston
16.5.88	Thurnscoe	1.10.90	Woodsmoor
16.5.88	Newbury Racecourse	2.10.90	Bloxwich North (X)
20. 6.88	Falls of Cruachan		
12. 7.88	Outwood	19. 3.91	Stansted Airport
16. 8.88	Overpool	12. 4.91	Hawkhead (X)
1.10.88	Arlesley	13. 5.91	Kirk Sandall
3.10.88	Musselburgh	27. 5.91	New Cumnock
3.10.88	Martins Heron	20. 7.91	Smallbrook Junction
3.10.88	Abercynon North		
3.10.88	Aberdare	27. 4.92	Bentley
3.10.88	Cwmbach	11. 5.92	Featherstone (X)
3.10.88	Fernhill	11. 5.92	Pontefract Tanshelf (X)
3.10.88	Mountain Ash	11. 5.92	Streethouse (X)
3.10.88	Penrhiwceiber	11. 5.92	Pencoed
22.10.88	How Wood	11. 5.92	Glenrothes with Thornton
28.11.88	Lichfield T.V.H.L.	24. 8.92	Hornbeam Park
28.11.88	Burley Park	28. 9.92	Pontyclun

28.	9.92	Maesteg Castle Street	1. 6.94	Briton Ferry (X)

28. 9.92   Maesteg Castle Street
28. 9.92   Sarn
28. 9.92   Tondu
28. 9.92   Garth
18.11.92   Maesteg Ewenny Road
18.11.92   Wildmill
21.12.92   Whifflet

8. 5.93   Hucknall
8. 5.93   Newstead
17. 5.93   Manchester Airport
20. 9.93   Gretna Green
4.10.93   Kirkwood
4.10.93   Bargeddie
4.10.93   Baillieston
4.10.93   Mount Vernon
4.10.93   Carmyle
11.10.93   Adwick
3.12.93   Maryhill.
3.12.93   Summerston
3.12.93   Lambhill
3.12.93   Ashfield
3.12.93   Possilpark & Parkhouse

27. 5.94   Bullwell (X)
27. 5.94   Barrow on Soar (X)
27. 5.94   Sileby (X)
27. 5.94   Syston (X)
29. 5.94   Cam & Dursley (X)
29. 5.94   Ramsgreave and Wilpshire (X)
29. 5.94   Whalley (X)
29. 5.94   Langho (X)

1. 6.94   Briton Ferry (X)
13. 6.94   Wallyford
27. 6.94   Llansamlet (X)
27. 6.94   Sanquhar
27. 6.94   Skewen (X)
27. 6.94   Pyle (X)
14. 7.94   Ivybridge
5. 9.94   Prestwick International Airport
27. 9.94   Camelon

3. 4.95   Eastham Rake
23. 5.95   Digby & Sowton (X)
26. 5.95   Willington
30. 5.95   Chafford Hundred
24. 9.95   Jewellery Quarter
24. 9.95   The Hawthorns
24. 9.95   Smethwick Galton Bridge
20.11.95   Sutton Parkway
20.11.95   Mansfield
20.11.95   Mansfield Woodhouse

20. 2.96   Yarm (X)
11. 3.96   Filton Abbey Wood
3. 6.96   Baglan
17.11.96   Kirkby in Ashfield (X)

25. 5.97   Okehampton
1. 6.97   Ashchurch
1. 6.97   Rugeley Town (X)
15.12.97   Euxton Balshaw Lane (X)

9. 3.98   Brunswick

Stations due in 1998

Brunswick,	Merseyside
Conway Park,	Merseyside
Wavertree Technical Park,	Merseyside
Dalgety Bay,	Fife
Drumfrochar,	Inverclyde
Creswell Langwith-Whaley Thorns Whitwell Shirebrook	} Derbyshire
Luton Parkway,	Bedfordshire.
Heathrow Central Heathrow Terminal 4	} London
West Ham	London

Stations planned for 1999

Addenbrookes Hospital,	Cambridge
Brighouse Elland	} West Yorks
Coleshill,	Warwickshire
Ferniegair Merryton Larkhall	} Strathclyde
Warwick Parkway	Warwickshire.
Horwich Parkway	Greater Manchester

Miscellaneous Station Openings

Opened & Closed

CORBY: This station opened on 13.4.87 but due to an irregular timetable for a Corby – Kettering shuttle and the use of unreliable 30 year old diesel trains the patronage was insufficient to cover the operating costs. The Councils were unwilling to assist with funding and the experimental service ceased on 4th June 1990.

SINFIN NORTH & CENTRAL: Opened on 4.10.76 on a 1 mile single branch line south of Derby, these stations only enjoyed 2 peak hour trains per day exclusively for employees of adjacent industries, The trains ceased in 1993 on the grounds that Sprinter trains did not actuate the low voltage track circuits and taxis were substituted. In December 1997 formal closure notices were published.

Relocated Stations

ALVECHURCH	19. 3.93	Relocated north of a substandard facility.
ARDROSSAN HARBOUR	15. 6.87	Moved 100 metres to avoid a level crossing.
BACHE, Cheshire	9. 1.84	£145,000 station replaced Upton on Chester.
BALLOCH	24. 4.88	Relocated to avoid a level crossing.
BILLINGHAM	7.11.86	Relocated 1 mile east.
BLACKHORSE ROAD, London	14.12.81	Relocated to west side of road bridge.
BLAENAU FFESTINIOG	22. 3.82	Moved to provide interchange with Steam Railway.
BRADFORD INTERCHANGE	11. 6.90	Resited 200 metres for new bus station.
BRIDGETON (Glasgow)	5.11.79	Replaced Bridgeton Central.
CHAPELTOWN (S.Yorks)	2. 8.82	Moved 200 metres nearer town centre.
ELTHAM, London	17. 3.85	Replaced Eltham Park and Eltham Well Hall.
FORT WILLIAM	9. 6.75	Relocated northwards due to redevelopment.
GODLEY, Gtr Manchester	7. 7.86	Opened 20 chains west of Godley East.
GUNNISLAKE, Cornwall	22. 6.94	Moved 25 chains south.
MORECAMBE	22. 5.94	Resited 400 yds for sea front development.
PARTICK, Glasgow	17.12.79	Moved 50 chains east to improve interchange.
POLEGATE, Eastbourne	25 5.86	Moved 40 chains west on Lewes line.
REDDITCH	7 2.72	Moved northwards to relocate bus station.
SANDWELL & DUDLEY	16. 5.83	Replaced Oldbury station on same site.
SUDBURY	29.10.91	Relocated.
UCKFIELD, E Sussex	13. 5.91	Relocated to north of level crossing.
WREXHAM CENTRAL	1998	Moving 280 metres west for a shopping development

Temporary Stations

AIRPORT JUNCTION	19.1.98	In use until completion of tunnel to Heathrow.
COALBROOKDALE	30.6.87– Sept 1990	For visitors to Ironbridge Museum.
CHEE DALE (Derbyshire)	57.87– 1991	Opened for Peak rail ramblers.
MAENTWROG ROAD	17.7.89– 1990	For visitors to Trawsfynydd.
MEADOWBANK (Edinburgh)	14.6.86– 23. 6.86	For Commonwealth Games visitors.
OVER (Gloucester)	8.2.90	An emergency platform due to flooding.
STANHOPE (Co Durham)	22.5.88– 1992	For visitors to Upper Weardale.
WITTON PARK (Co Durham)	25.8.91– 1992	For visitors to Upper Weardale.

KIRBY IN ASHFIELD, Notts. Opened 17.11.96   Photo: Central Trains

LANGHO, Near Clitheroe, Lancs. Opened 29.5.94   Photo: Brian Haworth

Chapter 3

NEW LINES FOR PASSENGERS

In addition to the many stations opened along existing passenger routes, an increasing number of services have been introduced on former freight-only lines or via newly constructed tracks. Those opened experimentally are marked (X).

FREIGHT LINES REOPENED TO PASSENGER SERVICES

Barassie – Kilmarnock	13 miles		5.69
Peterborough – Spalding	15 miles		7. 6.71
Perth – Ladybank	20 miles		6.10.75
Derby – Sinfin	2 miles		4.10.76
Leamington Spa – Coventry	10 miles		2. 5.77
Glasgow "Argyle" Line	5 miles		5.11.79
Penistone – Barnsley	7 miles (X)		16. 5.83
Dalston – Stratford	3 miles		17. 5.83
Blaydon – Dunston – Newcastle	4 miles		1.10.84
Burnley – Todmorden	10 miles		1.10.84
Cardiff "City" Line	5 miles (X)		11. 5.85
Bathgate – Edinburgh	10 miles (X)		24. 3.86
Addleston – Byfleet curve	0.5 miles		12. 5.86
Kensington – Willesden	3 miles		12. 5.86
Corby – Kettering	5 miles (X)	13. 4.87 to	4. 6.90
Oxford – Bicester Town	10 miles (X)		9. 5.87
Coventry – Nuneaton	10 miles (X)		11. 5.87
Rotherham Central J. – Aldwarke J.	2 miles		11. 5.87
Heysham – Morecambe	4 miles (X)		11. 5.87
Didcot North J. – Foxhall J.	0.5 miles (X)		16. 5.88
Aberdare – Abercynon	7 miles		3.10.88
Lichfield City – Lichfield T.V.H.L.	1 mile (X)		28.11.88
Walsall – Hednesford	10 miles (X)		8. 4.89
Timperley – Stockport	7 miles (X)		15. 5.89
Syston N.E. curve (Leicester)	0.5 miles		14. 5.90
Blackburn – Clitheroe	10 miles		19. 5.90
Glasgow – Paisley Canal	6 miles		30. 7.90
Inverkeithing N-E curve	0.37 miles		5. 1.92
Wakefield – Pontefract	8.5 miles		11. 5.92
Bridgend – Maesteg	8 miles		28. 9.93
Nottingham – Newstead	10.75 miles		8. 5.93

Freight lines reopened to passenger services (Continued)

Rutherglen – Whifflet	7.25 miles	4.10.93
Glasgow Queen Street – Maryhill	3 miles	6.12.93
Bristol (N-E) Loop	23 chains (X)	29. 5.94
Liverpool Curve, Earlstown	20 chains (X)	29. 5.94
Mitre Bridge Curve, London	43 chains (X)	29. 5.94
Sheepcote Lane Curve, London	17 chains (X)	29. 5.94
Kirkby – Mansfield	5 miles	20.11.95
Middlesbrough – Northallerton	14.5 miles	20. 2.96
Coatbridge Central – Greenfaulds	2.25 miles	27. 5.96
Linlithgow – Dalmeny	4.25 miles (X)	3. 6.96
Crediton – Okehampton	18 miles	25. 5.97
Hednesford – Rugeley Town	4 miles (X)	1. 6.97

Lines expected to reopen

Rugeley Town – Trent Valley	1 mile	June 1998
Walsall – Wolverhampton	6 miles	June 1998
Mansfield – Worksop	13 miles	June 1998
Halifax – Huddersfield	7 miles	Mid 1999
Leicester – Ashby	20 miles	Late 1999

NEWLY CONSTRUCTED LINES FOR PASSENGER TRAINS

Liverpool underground loop and north-south lines	3 miles	3. 2.77
Selby East Coast Main Line Deviation	12 miles	3.10.83
Stockport Hazel Grove chord	0.37 miles	12. 5.86
Rotherham, "Holmes Chord" link	0.75 miles	11. 5.87
Birmingham Snow Hill – Moor Street reinstatement	0.75 miles	5.10.87
Farringdon – Blackfriars reinstatement	1 mile	16. 5.88
Salford Cres. – Ordsall Ln (Windsor Link)	0.5 miles	16. 5.88
Airdrie – Drumgelloch extension	1.5 miles	16. 5.89
Swinton curve	0.5 miles	17. 3.90
Stansted Airport Link	3.5 miles	10. 3.91
Waterloo Curve Stewarts Lane Viaduct	1,000 metres	Nov. 92
Manchester Airport Link	1.5 miles	17. 5.93
Cowlairs Chord	600 metres	Oct. 1993
Channel Tunnel	20 miles	14.11.94
Snow Hill – Smethwick West reinstatement	4 miles	24. 9.95
Newstead – Kirkby	3 miles	20.11.95
Manchester Airport South curve	750 metres	15. 1.96
Heathrow Airport – Hayes	4 miles	mid-1998

LLANSAMLET, on the S. Wales main line. 12.7.94   Photo: Rhodri Clark

MAESTEG EWENNY RD, South Wales.   15.4.93   Photo: Rhodri Clark

MANCHESTER AIRPORT.   Opened 17.5.93   Photo: G.M.P.T.E.

MANSFIELD, on the Robin Hood Line.   April 1996   Photo: Peter Cannon

Chapter 4

SEEKING RAIL RE-OPENINGS

As the nation collectively enthuses over the need to reduce road traffic congestion, diesel pollution and road building, and to secure the integration and improvement of public transport, one would expect the opening of new stations and train services would become an increasing and priority activity. Sadly the reverse is now the case!

Problems

The endeavours of rail promoters are still beset by car owning sceptics, the evaporation of capital funding and endless difficulties arising from a fragmented railway. Despite government guidelines on route protection for future rail re-openings the formations still fall prey to new housing and road schemes. Reorganisation in local government and the railway industry has brought inertia and delays. The drastic curtailment of train building; the new train leasing and track access obligations; and the new franchise constraints has also put severe restrictions on the ability to provide new train services. No central strategy or responsibility exists towards rail expansion and consequently, after prolonged stop-go gestation, very few rail schemes have proceeded. Even in the conurbations only a limited number of rail schemes are being implemented. Rail promoters are, more than ever, obliged to draw heavily on their persistence and conviction that rail can, and eventually must, secure a greater role in our economic and environmental well-being.

Costs

Stringent safety requirements, new mobility regulations, signal and track constraints and contracting procedures amongst the new private rail companies has caused costs to escalate dramatically. Stations alone now generally cost four times the amount required a decade ago. The requirement for all new stations to have full mobility standard access ramps plus full width and longer than the trains platforms has doubled costs in the last 12 months. On operational lines the need for "look-out" men and sometimes track possessions is also imposing higher cost burdens. For over a decade new rail projects have been excluded from Transport Supplementary Grant funding and only those capital projects in excess of £5m may enjoy the daunting task of aspiring to a Section 56 grant – where it can be shown that non-rail users will benefit! Railtrack, which stands to gain in the long term, does not normally accept it as their role to finance a new station and only proceeds where others provide the majority funding. The franchising of train operating companies has also brought major difficulties. Having set the new Passenger Service Requirement and agreed the funding arrangements the Franchise Director has been precluded from adding any subsequent train services unless they are guaranteed financial support from other sources or are adopted as commercial ventures. Although Train Operating Companies are free to supplement their franchises with commercial ventures OPRAF will not risk new revenue support for "experimental" services with savings taken from "profitable" routes. Many rail reopenings are thus at a standstill. One recent concession however is acceptance that social and environmental benefits will be taken into account towards achieving a cost neutral rail service. Clearly the future expansion of rail services calls for a new financial policy

Success
Rail campaigners have of course been much encouraged by the realisation and success of earlier re-opening schemes. In London, agitation to make use of an abandoned 1 mile subterranean passage eventually secured the re-opening in 1988 of what is now the highly successful Thames-Link route via Farringdon and Blackfriars. In Scotland a campaign to bring passenger trains to a 10 mile route linking Edinburgh and Bathgate gained new services in 1986 which were estimated to carry 278,000 passenger journeys per annum rising to 335,000 in 1990. However the volumes were actually 500,000 and 932,000 respectively! Although passenger numbers are now often claimed to be "commercially sensitive" it is known that trains reintroduced between Glasgow – Paisley Canal; Walsall – Hednesford, the Rugeley extension; Aberdare – Cardiff; Nottingham – Newstead and elsewhere have also exceeded expectations. Overcrowded trains on these re-opened lines have of course obliged operators to provide longer trains and to increase frequencies.

Benefits
The value of opening new stations and train services is the very real and wider social, economic and environmental benefits. New rail services do attract motorists off congested urban roads by offering fast, smooth transit and often the convenience of a free local car park. Trains are particularly convenient for those with pushchairs, bicycles or impaired mobility. New train services are often able to offer new access for employment, shopping, leisure or tourists; and sometimes significantly aid urban regeneration and development. The value of local property and commerce is usually enhanced by new train services. Where links are made with other rail services their viability inevitably gains from increased use of the network. Re-opened lines can also create beneficial links with heritage railways and facilitate new freight opportunities.

Burdens

Transport Authorities, Councils, T.O.C.'s, EWSR and even Railtrack are all being seriously handicapped by current policies which frustrate endeavours to develop the rail network. The British Rail subsidiary Rail Property plc, which owns non-operational ex-railway land is racing ahead with its mission to sell-off station sites and rail routes, including those known to be the subject of firm reopening proposals. Even major players like EWSR and Railtrack are having to hurriedly negotiate the purchase of strategic parcels of land for new rail developments. Hundreds of miles of trackbeds may also be acquired by Sustrans for cycle paths, again including routes sought for reopened rail services and in addition to requiring the new cyclepaths to be relocated not all schemes can physically or safely accommodate one or two tracks alongside. Where tracks have been removed rail reopening schemes are also burdened with the need to obtain an order under the Transport & Works Act 1992 even where the trackbed is entirely available for immediate reinstatement. The TWA order requirement entails public consultations, a possible public enquiry and delays of up to 2-3 years. Another burden is the occasional need to provide an Environmental Impact Assessment and although railways are well able to satisfy modern day requirements the studies are an additional cost and time constraint to rail reopening projects.

Strategy

Reduced traffic volumes, congestion, pollution and car dependency are all essential targets for the millennium and rail clearly has the ability to attract and carry far more passengers and freight traffic in a sustainable and environmentally acceptable manner. A firm national commitment and strategy is essential to achieve the expansion of rail services. This should include greater protection of routes proposed for reinstated train services and the provision of specific grants for rail developments. Where firm agreement exists for a rail scheme it should not be necessary to examine or adopt inferior busways. Investment in rail schemes should take into account the environmental and social benefits. Also Railtrack, whose property and income would be enhanced, should be a major contributor to and initiate station and line re-openings – as indeed could the rail freight operator EWSR. The artificial exclusion of "introductory" funding for new services must be revised and scope for the virement of franchise surpluses should be considered to overcome the reopenings "standstill". Current financial policies and regulatory constraints will have to be addressed in order to achieve a new and positive framework which will encourage and enable essential and beneficial new railway developments to take place. A great many hopes and expectations now rest on the forthcoming Transport review and the intended Strategic Rail Authority.

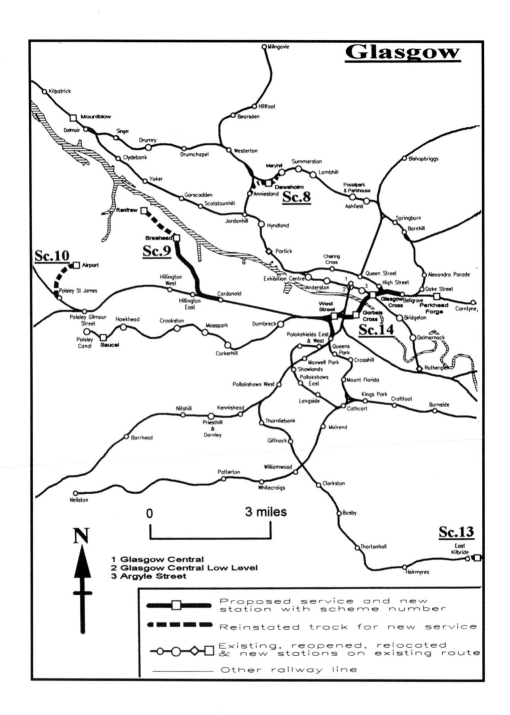

Glasgow

Milngavie
Kilpatrick
Hillfoot
Mountblow
Dalmuir
Bearsden
Singer
Drumry
Clydebank
Drumchapel
Westerton
Bishopbriggs
Yoker
Maryhill
Summerston
Lambhill
Gorscadden
Dawsholm **Sc.8**
Anniesland
Possilpark & Parkhouse
Scotstounhill
Renfrew
Ashfield
Jordanhill
Hyndland
Springburn
Braehead **Sc.9**
Barnhill
Sc.10 Airport
Partick
Charing Cross
Queen Street
Alexandra Parade
Hillington West
Exhibition Centre
Anderston
High Street
Duke Street
Paisley St James
Cardonald
1
3
Glasgow Cross
Belgrove
Parkhead Forge
Paisley Gilmour Street
Hillington East
2
West Street
Gorbals Cross
Bridgeton
Carntyne
Hawkhead
Crookston
Mosspark
Dumbreck
Sc.14
Daimarnock
Paisley Canal **Saucel**
Corkerhill
Polokshields East & West
Queens Park
Crosshill
Rutherglen
Maxwell Park
Shawlands
Pollokshaws West
Pollokshaws East
Mount Florida
Nitshill
Kennishead
Langside
Kings Park
Croftfoot
Burnside
Priesthill & Darnley
Thornliebank
Cathcart
Barrhead
Muirend
Giffnock
Patterton
Williamwood
Neilston
Whitecraigs
Clarkston
Busby
Sc.13 East Kilbride
Thorntonhall
Hairmyres

0   **3 miles**

N

1 Glasgow Central
2 Glasgow Central Low Level
3 Argyle Street

Proposed service and new station with scheme number

Reinstated track for new service

Existing, reopened, relocated & new stations on existing route

Other railway line

Chapter 5

PROPOSED LINES AND STATIONS

A host of proposed passenger lines and stations are summarised in this Chapter and are grouped into five broad areas, namely Scotland, Northern England, Central England, Wales and South West, and South-East England.

SCOTLAND

Sc.1   DORNOCH CROSSING, Highland.

The "Lairg Loop" was originally built by the Duke of Sutherland to help develop his estate but it now puts the railway at a serious 30 mile disadvantage to the road competition. A plan to build a short-cut across the Dornoch Firth has been around for many years. ScotRail were ready to start but when the road crossing was being built the Scottish Office refused to fund a rail link alongside. However Railway campaigners and local authorities still aim to secure a rail bridge across the Dornoch Firth. The railway would leave the present line near Tain and parallel the road crossing. A station is planned at Dornoch, the largest town in the area, whose original station closed in 1960.

Sc.2   ST ANDREWS – LEUCHARS, Fife.

Visitors to the world famous St Andrews golf courses; tourists to the historic city; students at the University and commuters and shoppers to Dundee or Edinburgh would all benefit from the restoration of train services to the 5 mile long branch.

Sc.3   THORNTON – METHIL, Fife.

Restoring passenger services to this freight-only line would allow travellers to reach Edinburgh in half the 1 hr 50 mins required by road. The £2.0 million scheme has been delayed by rail and local government reorganisation and a shortage of trains but it is expected that the local authority will restart the plan once the Fife Circle services have been upgraded.

Sc.4   STIRLING – ALLOA, Stirlingshire, Clackmannanshire.

Reopening of this 6 mile freight line had been agreed in 1991 but subsequent "technical" issues and reorganisations caused postponement. Alloa is the largest community in Scotland not on the rail network and reopening of the line with three new stations remains a high aspiration.

Sc.5   ALLOA – DUNFERMLINE, Clackmannanshire, Fife.

With the exception of one or two missing lengths the rails are still in-situ between Stirling and Dunfermline via Alloa. The line is in use for coal trains between Dunfermline and Longannet power station and maintained useable from there to Kincardine Power Station. Restoration of passenger services would be sought as a follow-on to a Stirling – Alloa reopening.

Sc.6   FALKIRK – GRANGEMOUTH, Falkirk.

The 2 mile freight-only line from Falkirk to Grangemouth is planned to be re-opened to passengers as an extension of Glasgow to Falkirk Grahamston services utilising turnaround times of existing trains. Under the former Central Regional Council plans were well advanced but rail privatisation and local government reorganisation has caused the project to be postponed.

Sc.7   LENZIE – KIRKINTILLOCH – MILTON OF CAMPSIE, East Dunbartonshire.

A 3 mile re-instatement along a fairly well preserved trackbed from the junction off the Glasgow Queen Street to Falkirk Line at Lenzie. This would serve an area of serious potential traffic growth with a poor and congested road system. It is at a very early planning stage and is supported by Strathclyde PTA and ScotRail.

Sc.8   MARYHILL – ANNIESLAND EXTENSION, Glasgow.

The Northern Suburban service using diesel multiple units opened in December 1993. Viability for the service requires that the proposed extension to Anniesland is completed. This requires reinstatement of a 1,570 metre spur, a new station at Dawsholm and a bay platform at Anniesland where passengers can connect with electric services.

Sc.9   GLASGOW – RENFREW, Renfrewshire.

A 2.5 mile re-instatement of track is proposed from Glasgow –Paisley Line at Cardonald partly following freight sidings and partly protected trackbed via a major "out of town" shopping and commercial development at Braehead to Renfrew.

Sc.10 GLASGOW AIRPORT, Renfrewshire.

A new 1.5 mile rail link is advocated to Glasgow Airport for its 6 million annual passengers. Diverting off the Gourock line at Paisley St James the line would link direct with the Airport Terminal.

Sc.11 KILMACOLM – PAISLEY, Inverclyde, Renfrewshire.

Closed as recently as 1983 the former Kilmacolm Line had already been re-opened as far as Paisley Canal by 1990! Development across the track prevented further re-opening but a junction off the Ayr Line at Elderslie would give much higher speed access to the remainder of the Kilmacolm Line. The 7 mile line would have stations at Linwood, Bridge of Weir and Kilmacolm and serve what has now become a high car journey generation area.

Sc.12 AYR – ALLOWAY – GREENAN, South Ayrshire.

Re-opening of a three mile section of the former coastal route south of Ayr is endorsed by Strathclyde P.T.A. The old trackbed would be reinstated and electrified with stations at Alloway for housing developments and Tam O'Shanter Centre, and at Greenan for Wonderwest World Holiday Centre. Increased utilisation of Ayr Line trains would provide the rolling stock.

Sc.13 EAST KILBRIDE TOWN CENTRE EXTENSION, South Lanarkshire.

East Kilbride New Town was designed without much reference to the part that railways could play and the East Kilbride Line terminates half a mile from the thriving commercial and shopping centre. An extension was planned by Strathclyde PTA to an underground station beneath the town centre and finance was allocated but then the Scottish Office rejected the scheme. The plan is presently in abeyance but the problems mount for congestion in East Kilbride, not just to the centre but to the road served "Silicon Park" employment area to the South East of the town and for connections to nearby Hamilton which has become the centre for the new Council administration.

Sc.14 GLASGOW CROSSRAIL, Glasgow.

In modern times the passenger rail systems of the South and North of Glasgow have been isolated from each other by the River Clyde despite there being a connecting line which is only used for stock movements. This line uses the former Glasgow St Enoch approach bridge over the Clyde and plans are in hand to run passenger services over this bridge from South West to North Glasgow, suburban trains at first but then possibly ScotRail services linking, for example, Ayr with Aberdeen. Most of the infrastructure is in place but spurs are required at either end of the link, at High Street and West Street. The cost is of the order of £35 million and some of the design is very difficult because station sites having to be squeezed into confined areas. The Crossrail scheme will enable many new and better journey opportunities across the entire suburban system.

Sc.15 CUMBERNAULD – FALKIRK/STIRLING, North Lanarkshire, Falkirk.

Use of the 5 miles of existing main line north of Cumbernauld in Central Scotland is sought for the extension of Motherwell and Coatbridge services to Larbert and Stirling, thus avoiding circuitous and time consuming journeys via Glasgow. The extension of Glasgow – Stepps – Cumbernauld trains is also sought to Falkirk.

Sc.16 AIRDRIE – BATHGATE, North Lanarkshire, West Lothian.

The re-opening of the Bathgate Line has been a resounding success and the extension of the Airdrie Line to Drumgelloch paid for itself in its first year. Only 12 miles of intact trackbed separates Bathgate from Drumgelloch and restoration of this link would provide journey opportunities for Airdrie to Edinburgh and from the Bathgate area to Glasgow. Journey opportunities which are almost impossible at present. Several small former mining towns with very high unemployment rates are located along the route at Plains, Caldercruix, Blackridge and Armadale. The trackbed has been kept intact because there is thought to be considerable mineral traffic potential although a cycle track has been built using part of the trackbed.

Sc.17 HAMILTON TO LARKHALL, South Lanarkshire.

Restoration of a three mile rail link closed in 1965 would bring Larkhall, with a population of 14,000, back on to the rail system. The link would start at Haughead Junction on the Hamilton Circle and would be a single electrified track. Intermediate stations are planned for Ferniegair, near to Chatelherhault Country Park and at Merryton for new housing developments. In January 1998 Strathclyde PTA were hoping to finalise the £23m scheme with Railtrack and contributions from EC grants, private finance and Challenge funding for a completion in mid-2000.

Sc.18 LANARK CHORD, South Lanarkshire.

Lanark and the surrounding area lost its rail services to Edinburgh, 33 miles away, in 1965 and the southern chord of the triangular junction from Lanark was dismantled. The people of Lanark have continued to campaign for train services to Edinburgh and a recent extension to the boundaries of Strathclyde PTA has made this administratively possible. The chord cannot be reinstated on the exact original line as houses have been built on the trackbed but a slightly different line is possible. The reinstatement of this chord would allow very competitive journey times to the Scottish Capital; existing Glasgow – Lanark trains to be extended to Edinburgh; and would ease congestion on the mainline caused by coal trains having to run "wrong line" from the nearby Ravenstruther Coal Terminal.

Sc.19 EDINBURGH SOUTH SUBURBAN CIRCLE, Edinburgh.

The 7.5 mile Edinburgh freight-only loop is available for restoring a suburban rail service to a total of 15 stations. The route is circumferential rather than radial but still offers quicker journeys than radial road routes.

Sc.20 EDINBURGH – GALASHIELS, Midlothian, Scottish Borders.

This project is envisaged in two parts. First, a service for the built-up and congested area around Dalkeith into Edinburgh and secondly an extension to a railhead at Galashiels in the presently rail-less Scottish Borders region. While much of the trackbed is intact there is some severance particularly at he Edinburgh City By-pass. A private company, Border Transport Futures, has been formed to work through all the problems and possible funding for relaying the track and restarting services. The same company is also developing a plan for a freight, mainly timber, line at the southern end of the former Waverley Line from Carlisle to Kielder.

Sc.21 DUMFRIES – STRANRAER, Dumfries & Galloway.

Closure of the 72 miles of the direct Port Line between Dumfries and Stranraer in 1965 left the railway with an extra 53 mile detour via Kilmarnock. In 1991 local councils and the European Commission had an interest in re-opening the line to give better transport links with Ireland. The short sea route via Stranraer and Larne had increased to 30 sailings a day and continues to be improved with larger vessels and faster SeaCat vessels. The Reinstatement could cost £150–£200m depending on how much damage has been done to the solum. There is still no focus on whether a reinstated line should attempt to serve local towns or stay well away from them to provide the cheapest reconstruction costs.

Proposed Stations in Scotland

County/Station	Line	County/Station	Line
ABEREDEEN		**CLACKMANNANSHIRE**	
Persley	} Aberdeen – Inverness	Alloa	} Stirling – Dunfermline
Schoolhill		Cambus	Sc4
		Clackmannan	
Tullos	} Aberdeen – Edinburgh		
Altens		**DUMFRIES & GALLOWAY**	
Cove		Beattock	Lockerbie – Carstairs
		DUNBARTONSHIRE	
ABERDEENSHIRE		Mountblow	Glasgow – Helensburgh
Kintore	Aberdeen – Inverness	**EAST AYRSHIRE**	
Newtonhill	} Aberdeen – Inverness	Hurlford	} Glasgow – Dumfries
Laurencekirk		Mauchline	

County/Station	Line
EAST DUNBARTONSHIRE	
Kirkintilloch Milton of Campsie }	Milton of Campsie Sc7
EDINBURGH	
Edinburgh Park	Edinburgh – Glasgow
Asda, The Jewel Niddrie Craigmillar Cameron Toll Newington Blackford Morningside Craiglockhart Gorgie }	Edinburgh South Suburban Circle S19
Winchburgh	Edinburgh – Stirling
Cogar	Edinburgh – Dundee
FALKIRK	
Grangemouth	Grangemouth – Falkirk
FIFE	
Culross Kincardine Low Valleyfield }	Stirling – Dunfermline Sc5
Dunfermline East	Fife Circle
Newburgh	Edinburgh – Perth
Dysart/Sinclairston Wormit }	Edinburgh – Dundee
St Andrews	Leuchars Sc2
Cameron Bridge Leven }	Thornton – Methil Sc3
GLASGOW	
Parkhead Forge	Glasgow – Airdrie
Glasgow Cross Gorbals Cross West Street }	Glasgow Crossrail Sc14
Dawsholm	Maryhill – Anniesland Sc8
HIGHLAND	
Beauly Evanton Halkirk Dornoch Embo }	Inverness – Wick Far North Line Sc1

County/Station	Line
MIDLOTHIAN	
Newcraighill Millerhill Eskbank (Dalkkeith) Newtongrange Gorebridge }	Edinburgh – Galashiels Sc20
NORTH LANARKSHIRE	
Gartcosh Millerston Glenboig }	Glasgow – Cumbernauld
Abronhill	Cumbernauld – Falkirk
Mossend (Calder Road) Viewpark }	Glasgow – Lanark
Mossend (Eurocentral)	Motherwell – Cumbernauld
Armadale Caldercruix Plains }	Bathgate – Drumgelloch Sc16
PERTH – KINROSS	
Bridge of Earn Abernethy }	Edinburgh – Perth
Blackford	Stirling – Perth
RENFREWSHIRE	
Braehead Renfrew }	Glasgow – Renfrew Sc9
Saucel	Glasgow – Paisley Canal
Ferguslie Park Howwood }	Glasgow – Ayr
SCOTTISH BORDERS	
Galashiels	Edinburgh – Galashiels Sc20
SOUTH AYRSHIRE	
Belmont Carcluie Alloway Greenan }	Ayr – Greenan Sc12
Ayr Hospital	Ayr – Girvan
SOUTH LANARKSHIRE	
Ferniegair Merryton Larkhall }	Hamilton – Larkhall Sc17
Law Junction	Glasgow – Lanark
Symington Abington Crawford }	Carstairs – Carlisle
STIRLING	
Causewayhead	Stirling – Alloa Sc4

NORTHERN ENGLAND

N1   ALNMOUTH – ALNWICK, Northumberland

A local group, headed by the Duke of Northumberland, is promoting reinstatement of this 4 mile branch.

N2   ASHINGTON- NEWCASTLE UPON TYNE, Northumberland

The restoration of passenger services along the 15 mile freight route has been canvassed by the local Councils.   New stations are indicated at Ashington, North Seaton, Bedlington, West Blyth, Newsham and Seaton Delaval.

N3   PELAW – FERRYHILL, Tyne & Wear, Co Durham.

The 22 mile Leamside freight line is being considered by the Local Authorities for re-opening to a local passenger service with five stations not least to serve Washington New Town.   Other possible station sites are at Sulgrave, Barmston, Penshaw South and Fencehouses. The service could be extended south to Darlington.

N4   BISHOP AUCKLAND – EASTGATE, Co Durham.

Use of thie 20 mile freight line is being actively pursued not least to promote tourism into the scenic Weardale. Existing and new stations are planned at seven locations.

N5   PENRITH – KESWICK, Cumbria.

To reduce intrusive traffic and to benefit visitors to Lakeland the re-opening of this 15 mile line, closed in 1972, is being sought with up to 5 possible stations.

N6   NORTHALLERTON – WENSLEYDALE – GARSDALE, North Yorkshire.

The challenging task of re-opening this 40 mile route across the Yorkshire Dales NationaL Park is underway. From the East Coast main line the 22 miles of track to Redmire is in use by military trains. The remaining 18 miles to Garsdale on the Settle – Carlisle line requires longer-term reinstatement.

N7   HARROGATE – RIPON – NORTHALLERTON, North Yorkshire.

Reinstatement of this 24 mile rail route has strong local support. Most of the trackbed is intact but a new viaduct is required in Ripon due to the construction of a bypass. New stations are proposed for Bilton, Ripon, Melmerby and Pickhill.

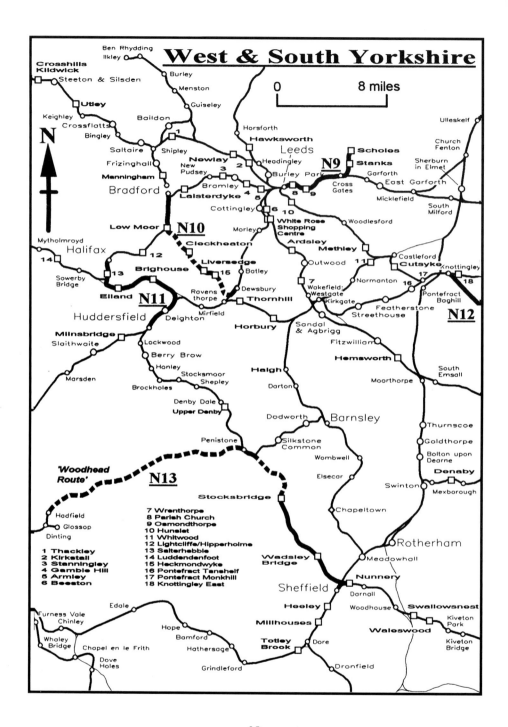

West & South Yorkshire

0   8 miles

N

Ben Rhydding
Ilkley
Crosshills
Kildwick
Steeton & Silsden
Burley
Menston
Utley
Guiseley
Keighley
Crossflatts
Baildon
Horsforth
Bingley
Hawksworth
Ulleskelf
Saltaire
Shipley
Leeds
Scholes
Church
Fenton
Frizinghall
Newlay
Headingley
N9
Stanks
Sherburn
in Elmet
New
Pudsey
Burley Park
Garforth
Manningham
Bradford
Bramley
Cross
Gates
East Garforth
Laisterdyke
Micklefield
Cottingley
South
Milford
Low Moor
N10
Morley
White Rose
Shopping
Centre
Woodlesford
Mytholmroyd
Cleckheaton
Ardsley
Methley
Halifax
12
Liversedge
Outwood
11
Castleford
Cutsyke
Knottingley
Sowerby
Bridge
Brighouse
Batley
Normanton
16
17
18
Elland
N11
Ravens
thorpe
Dewsbury
Thornhill
Wakefield
Westgate
Kirkgate
Pontefract
Baghill
N12
Huddersfield
Deighton
Mirfield
Horbury
Featherstone
Streethouse
Milnsbridge
Horbury
Sandal
& Agbrigg
Slaithwaite
Lockwood
Fitzwilliam
Berry Brow
Hemsworth
Honley
Stocksmoor
Haigh
South
Emsall
Marsden
Shepley
Darton
Moorthorpe
Brockholes
Denby Dale
Upper Denby
Dodworth
Barnsley
Thurnscoe
Penistone
Silkstone
Common
Goldthorpe
Wombwell
Bolton upon
Dearne
'Woodhead
Route'
N13
Elsecar
Denaby
Swinton
Mexborough
Stocksbridge
Hadfield
Chapeltown
Glossop
Dinting
Rotherham
1 Thackley
2 Kirkstall
3 Stanningley
4 Gamble Hill
5 Armley
6 Beeston
7 Wrenthorpe
8 Parish Church
9 Osmondthorpe
10 Hunslet
11 Whitwood
12 Lightcliffe/Hipperholme
13 Salterhebble
14 Luddendenfoot
15 Heckmondwyke
16 Pontefract Tanshelf
17 Pontefract Monkhill
18 Knottingley East
Wadsley
Bridge
Meadowhall
Nunnery
Sheffield
Furness Vale
Edale
Heeley
Woodhouse
Swallownest
Chinley
Millhouses
Waleswood
Kiveton
Park
Whaley
Bridge
Hope
Bamford
Totley
Brook
Dore
Kiveton
Bridge
Chapel en le Frith
Hathersage
Dove
Holes
Grindleford
Dronfield
Darnall

N8 CLITHEROE – HELLIFIELD, Lancashire.

Folowing on from the succesful re-opening of the Blackburn – Clitheroe line with three intermediate stations, endeavours and studies are being made towards extending train services northwards to Hellifield to connect with services to Leeds, Carnforth and Carlisle

N9 LEEDS – SCHOLES, West Yorkshire

Along with new stations at Parish Church and Osmondthorpe the re-use of the 2 mile Cross Gates – Stanks – Scholes branch is being proposed for rail services to and from Leeds.

N10 BRADFORD – DEWSBURY, West Yorkshire.

The reinstatement of the 6 mile Spen Valley route with stations at Cleckheaton, Liversedge and Heckmondwike is sought, requiring a new connection at the Dewsbury end.

N11 HALIFAX – HUDDERSFIELD, West Yorkshire.

Re-opening of this 7 mile freight line to passenger services is in hand for late 1999 with intermediate stations at Elland and Brighouse

N12 KNOTTINGLEY – DONCASTER, West & South Yorkshire.

Re-opening of the 10 mile freight line with a new station at Askern is proposed, possibly by extending existing Leeds – Knottingley services.

N13 HADFIELD – PENISTONE – SHEFFIELD, Derbyshire/South Yorkshire.

Several M.P.'s, Councils and study groups are endorsing pleas to re-open the 20 mile section of the Woodhead route. This once electrified route was closed in 1981 but is seen as an important freight route linking Humberside ports to the North-West and Ireland. Passenger services are also sought.

N14 HEYWOOD – CASTLETON, Greater Manchester.

A 2 mile extension of a freight line west of Castleton on the Rochdale – Manchester line is proposed to facilitate new passenger services to serve the town of Heywood and to provide an interchange with the East Lancashire Railway.

N15 BURSCOUGH CURVES, Lancashire.

Although two rail services "cross" north of Ormskirk there is no easy interchange or through services linking Southport with Preston or Ormskirk. Two short curves are sought to facilitate direct train services.

N16 RAINFORD – SKELMERSDALE, Lancashire.

A new 2 mile branch is sought from Rainford to Skelmersdale New Town on the former trackbed which could be served by an extension of the electric trains on the Liverpool – Kirkby route.

N17 BOOTLE – AINTREE, Merseyside.

Re-opening of the 2 mile freight line from Bootle to Aintree with intermediate stations serving the Girobank offices and Ainsworth Road is sought for this north Liverpool area.

N18 FRODSHAM – RUNCORN, Cheshire.

Retention and regular use of an important chord link is sought to facilitate a fast and direct Liverpool – Chester and North Wales service via Runcorn.

N19 NORTHWICH – SANDBACH, Cheshire.

Local Councils are supporting re-use of the 8 mile freight-only line which could provide a new Crewe – Manchester service via Northwich and a re-opened Middlewich station. A new station for Rudheath, south of Northwich is also sought.

Proposed Stations in Northern England

County/Station	Line	County/Station	Line
CHESHIRE		**DURHAM**	
Marshlands Road Neston	} Wrexham – Bidston	Horden and Peterlee	Newcastle – Middlesbrough
Middlewich Rudheath	} Northwich – Sandbach	Leamside Belmont Sherburn	} Pelaw – Ferry Hill, N3
Saltney	Chester – Wrexham		
Shaw Heath	Northwich – Altrincham	**GREATER MANCHESTER**	
Mickle Trafford	Chester – Warrington	Timperley East Baguley Cheadle Heath	} Timperley – Stockport
Beeston Castle Christleton	} Chester – Crewe		
Willaston	Crewe – Nantwich	Droylsden Clayton Vale Clayton Bridge Greenside	} Manchester – Stalybridge
Coppenhall Glazebury	Crewe – Winsford Patricroft – Newton le Willows		
Burtonwood	Warrington – Liverpool	Crossley Park Heaton Lane	} Manchester – Stockport
CUMBRIA		Dewsnap Diggle	Manchester – Glossop Manchester–Huddersfield
Cummersdale Gilsland	} Carlisle – Haltwhistle	Pendlebury Dobbs Brow	} Manchester – Wigan
Crosby Garrett Long Marton Newbiggin Little Salkeld Cumwhinton	} Settle – Carlisle	White City Horwich P/W	Manchester – Warrington Bolton – Preston

County/Station	Line	County/Station	Line
LANCASHIRE		**NORTHUMBERLAND**	
Bolton le Sands Carnforth Main Line }	Lancaster – Oxenholme	Ashington Green Lane North Seaton Bedlington West Blyth Newsham Seaton Delaval }	Newcastle – Ashington, N2
Chatburn Gisburn }	Clitheroe – Hellifield, N8		
Midge Hall Farrington Burscough South }	Ormskirk – Preston	South Cramlington	Cramlington – Newcastle
Hoghton Gregson Lane Blackburn Harwood Reedley Hollow Bott House Lane Lomeshave Walton Summit Gannow Junction Greenbank Nelson East }	Preston – Colne	**NORTH YORKSHIRE**	
		Lower Poppleton	Harrogate – York
		Copmanthorpe Dringhouses }	York – Church Fenton
		Cliffe Thorpe Willoughby	Selby – Hull Selby – Leeds
		Haxby Strensall Kirkham Priory }	York – Scarborough
Skelmersdale	Route N16	**SOUTH YORKSHIRE**	
Wrea Green St. Annes North Fairhaven Saltercoates }	South Fylde Line	Totley Brook Heeley Millhouses }	Sheffield – Edale
Lower Darwen Spring Vale Blackburn Infirmary }	Bolton – Blackburn	Denaby Finningley	Sheffield – Doncaster Doncaster–Gainsborough
Haslam Park Ashton on Ribble Cottam }	Blackpool – Preston	Nunnery Swallownest Waleswood }	Sheffield – Retford
		Askern	Doncaster–Knottingley (N12)
Coppull Leyland Church Rd. Galgate Bailrigg Garstang Catterall }	Wigan – Preston – Lancaster (WCML)	Rossington Bawtry }	Retford – Doncaster
		TEES-SIDE	
		Roseworth Hart }	Billingham – Middlesbrough
MERSEYSIDE		Middlehaven	Middlesbrough – Redcar
Town Meadow	Liverpool – West Kirkby	**TYNE AND WEAR**	
Prenton Woodchurch Ford }	Wrexham – Birkenhead	Killingworth Forest Hall Heaton }	Cramlington – Newcastle
Woodvale Vauxhall }	Liverpool – Southport	Bensham Team Valley Birtley }	Newcastle – Chester le Street
Ford Ainsworth Road }	Projected Route , N17	Washington Fencehouses }	Pelaw – Ferryhill, N3
Maghull North Headbolt Lane	Liverpool – Ormskirk Kirkby – Wigan	**WEST YORKSHIRE**	
Old Swan Huyton Quarry }	Liverpool – Earlestown	Leeds Parish Church Osmondthorpe }	Leeds – Cross Gates
Marshalls Cross	Liverpool – Manchester		
Otterspool	Liverpool – Hunts Cross		

County/Station	Line	County/Station	Line
Knottingley East Cutsyke }	Leeds – Goole	Armley Gamble Hill Stanningley Laisterdyke }	Leeds – Bradford
Methley Hunslet }	Leeds – Castleford	Manningham Charlestown }	Bradford – Ilkley
Whitwood Haigh }	Castleford – Barnsley	White Rose Centre	Leeds – Huddersfield/ Wakefield
Beeston Ardsley Wrenthorpe Hemsworth }	Leeds – Doncaster	Scholes Stanks }	New Line, N9
Upper Denby	Huddersfield – Penistone	Hawksworth Milnsbridge }	Leeds – Harrogate Huddersfield – Manchester
Elland Brighouse }	Halifax – Huddersfield, N11	Low Moor Lightcliffe/ Hipperholme Salterhebble Todmorden North Luddendenfoot }	Bradford – Burnley/Rochdale
Thornhill Horbury }	Wakefield – Huddersfield		
Crosshills Kildwick Utley }	Keighley – Skipton		
Thackley Newlay Kirkstall }	Leeds – Shipley	Cleckheaton Heckmondwike Liversedge }	Bradford – Dewsbury N10

CENTRAL ENGLAND

C1   BUXTON – MATLOCK, Derbyshire.

The re-opening of this 21 mile line for tourists, through passengers and freight is imaginative, feasible and environmentally desirable. The 5 mile Buxton – Millers Dale line is already open to freight and the 5 mile Matlock – Rowsley section is a steam heritage railway run by Peak Rail. The Peak Park Planning Board and others anxious to curtail road traffic are now investigating re-opening of the remaining 11 miles via Monsal Dale and Bakewell for passengers and for limestone freight.

C2   BURTON -ASHBY – LEICESTER, Derbyshire/Leicestershire.

The Phase II "Ivanhoe" line proposed 12 new stations including Kirby Muxloe, Coalville and Ashby along the 29 mile freight route. South of Leicester a new curve is planned to avoid reversing at Knighton. As ever costs are escalating and the Council are now planning a less extensive re-opening

C3 WALSALL – BROWNHILLS – LICHFIELD, West Midlands/Staffs.

Together with the use of the Wichnor – Lichfield – Brownhills freight line a 5 mile section of route from Brownhills to Walsall requires reinstatement in order to operate through trains, such as Derby-Burton-Lichfield-Walsall-Wolverhampton inter-urban services. A north – south service could also be linked to the Walsall – Dudley – Stourbridge line

C4 WALSALL – ALDRIDGE – CASTLE BROMWICH, West Midlands

This well used 11.5 mile freight route is a candidate for passenger trains serving Aldridge, Streetly, Sutton Coldfield, Walmley, Minworth, Castle Bromwich and Bromford. Aldridge alone warrants a rail service with Walsall.

C5 STOURBRIDGE -DUDLEY – WALSALL, West Midlands

Re-opening of the 12 mile Walsall -Dudley-Stourbridge freight line is sought for inter-urban passenger services and increasing freight services.. This north-south route traverses the heart of the "Black Country" with its intensive housing, industry and the vast Merry Hill shopping centre. An interim Walsall – Wednesbury shuttle is being sought for interchange with Midland Metro Line 1 which opens in late 1998.

C6 FRANKLEY – LONGBRIDGE, West Midlands

Utilising the track bed of the former Halesowen branch a scheme to serve the large Frankley housing estate is proposed as an extension of the "Cross-City" line. The initial mile is in use as sidings for the motor works. Beyond there are plans for a Rubery Park and Ride station and a terminus next to the Holly Hill shopping centre.

C7 STRATFORD ON AVON – HONEYBOURNE, Warwickshire/ Worcestershire

Apart from a 3 mile line from Honeybourne to Long Marston REME Depot the remaining 6 miles of the former main line to Stratford on Avon is devoid of track and mostly utilised as a walkway, with a 0.25 mile section alongside a new road. Restoration of a through rail link between Stratford on Avon and the Cotswold line is sought for tourist trains and for strategic benefits. Transport consultants have confirmed that re-opening is feasible.

C8 KETTERING – CORBY – LUFFENHAM, Northants/Rutland

A new chord link south of Manton Junction is proposed to facilitate Bedford – Kettering – Corby – Stamford – Peterborough services.

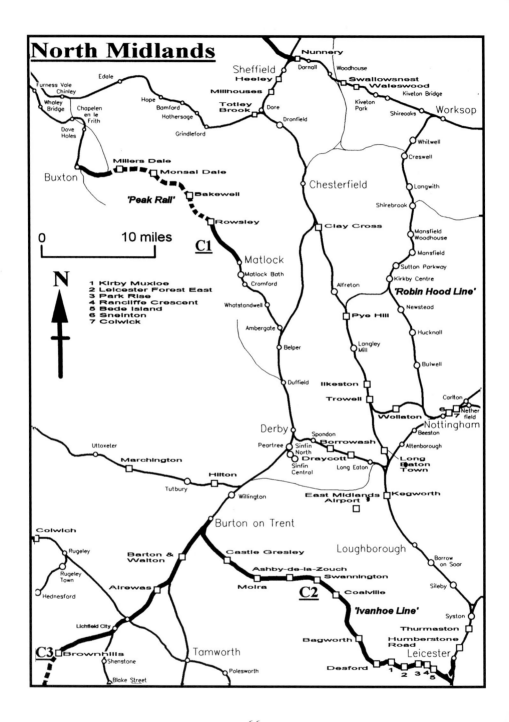

North Midlands

0   10 miles

N

1 Kirby Muxloe
2 Leicester Forest East
3 Park Rise
4 Rancliffe Crescent
5 Bede Island
6 Sneinton
7 Colwick

Furness Vale
Chinley
Edale
Wholey Bridge
Chapelen en le Frith
Dove Holes
Hope
Bamford
Hothersage
Grindleford

Sheffield
Heeley
Millhouses
Totley Brook
Dore
Dronfield

Nunnery
Dornall
Woodhouse
Swallowsnest
Waleswood
Kiveton Bridge
Kiveton Park
Shireoaks
Worksop

Millers Dale
Monsal Dale
Bakewell
'Peak Rail'
Rowsley
Buxton

Whitwell
Creswell
Langwith
Shirebrook

Chesterfield

Clay Cross

C1

Matlock
Matlock Bath
Cromford
Whatstandwell
Ambergate
Belper
Duffield

Alfreton

Pye Hill
Langley Mill

Ilkeston
Trowell

Mansfield Woodhouse
Mansfield
Sutton Parkway
Kirkby Centre
'Robin Hood Line'
Newstead
Hucknall
Bulwell

Carlton
6 Nether field
7
Wollaton
Nottingham
Beeston
Attenborough

Derby
Peartree
Spondon
Sinfin North
Draycott
Sinfin Central
Borrowash
Long Eaton
Long Eaton Town

Uttoxeter
Marchington
Hilton
Tutbury
Willington

East Midlands Airport
Kegworth

Burton on Trent
Loughborough
Barrow on Soar

Colwich
Rugeley
Rugeley Town
Hednesford
Alrewas

Barton & Walton
Castle Gresley
Ashby-de-la-Zouch
Moira
Swannington
C2
Coalville
Sileby

'Ivanhoe Line'

Lichfield City
C3 Brownhills
Shenstone
Blake Street
Tamworth
Polesworth

Bagworth
Desford

Syston
Thurmaston
Humberstone Road
Leicester
1 2 3 4 5

66

Proposed Stations in Central England

County/Station	Line	County/Station	Line
DERBYSHIRE		**LINCOLNSHIRE**	
Borrowash	} Derby – Trent Jn	Heighington	Lincoln – Sleaford
Draycott		Sibsey	Sleaford – Skegness
Pye Hill		Pinchbeck	
Clay Cross		Donington	
Ilkeston	Chesterfield – Nottingham	Helpringham	} Peterborough – Sleaford
Trowell		Deeping St.James	
Long Eaton Town			
		Moortown	
Castle Gresley	Burton – Leicester, C2	Cherry Willingham	} Lincoln – Barnetby
Hilton	Uttoxeter – Derby		
Gaimsley	Guide Bridge – Hadfield	Boultham	Lincoln – Newark
HEREFORD AND WORCESTER		**NORTHANTS**	
Malvern Wells		Corby	Kettering – Manton, C8
Rushwick	} Malvern – Worcester		
Henwick		**NOTTINGHAMSHIRE**	
		Misterton	Gainsborough-Doncaster
Fladbury	Worcester – Evesham	Wollaton	Nottingham-Chesterfield
Pontrilas	Hereford – Abergavenny	Sneiton	Nottingham – Carlton
		Colwick	Nottingham – Radcliffe
LEICESTERSHIRE		**SHROPSHIRE**	
Croft		Baschurch	
Blaby	} Nuneaton – Leicester	Whittington	} Shrewsbury – Chirk
Elmesthorpe		Weston Rhyn	
Thurmaston		**STAFFORDSHIRE**	
Humberstone Road		Alrewas	} Lichfield City – Burton
Rearsby		Barton and Walton	Projected Route, C3
Brooksby			
Frisby	} Leicester – Stamford	Marchington	Uttoxeter – Derby
Asfordby			
East Goscote		Fenton	}
Ketton		Meir	Uttoxeter – Stoke on Trent
		Dunston Parkway	Stafford – Penkridge
LEICESTERSHIRE		Brinsford Parkway	Penkridge –
Kegworth	Leicester – Trent Junction		Wolverhampton
		Trentham	Stone – Stoke on Trent
West Knighton			
Wigston Main Line	} Leicester – Kettering	Churchbridge Parkway	} Walsall – Rugeley
Kibworth		Hawkes Green	
Bede Island		Colwich	Stafford – Rugeley
Rancliffe Crescent			
Park Rise		**WARWICKSHIRE**	
Leicester Forest East		Kenilworth	Coventry –
Kirkby Muxloe	Leicester – Burton on		Leamington Spa
Desford	Trent Ivanhoe Line, C2	Coleshill	Water Orton – Nuneaton
Bagworth			
Coalville		Kingbury	} Water Orton – Tamworth
Swannington		Hams Hall	
Ashby de la Zouch			
Moira		Chilvers Coton	Nuneaton – Coventry
		Warwick Parkway	Solihull –
			Leamington Spa
		Bishops Itchington	Leamington – Banbury

County/Station	Line	County/Station	Line
WEST MIDLANDS		Foleshill	Coventry – Bedworth
Aldridge	⎫		
Streetly		Convention Centre	⎫
Sutton Park	Walsall – Castle	Summerfield	Birmingham –
Walmley	Bromwich Route C4.	Spring Vale	Wolverhampton
Minworth	⎭		⎭
		Bentley Heath	⎫
Bushbury	Wolverhampton –	Wadleys Road	Birmingham – Dorridge
	Stafford		⎭
		Round Oak	⎫
Heartlands	⎫	Dudley Castle	
Bromford		Dudley Port LL	Stourbridge – Walsall C5
Castle Vale	Birmingham –	Wednesbury	
	Water Orton		⎭

WALES

W1   AMLWCH – LLANFAIR, Anglesey

The restoration of passenger services along part of the 18 mile Amlwch freight line across the centre of Anglesey has been proposed using both steam and diesel traction. One former station at Llangefni could be re-opened en-route.

W2   CAERNARFON – BANGOR, Gwynedd

The relaying of 6 miles of track and the rebuilding of several bridges is envisaged in a £10m plan to restore train services from Bangor to Caernarfon. This would reduce road congestion, aid tourism to the castle, and link with the new West Highland Railway.

W3   SHOTTON CURVE, Flintshire

New curves are proposed at Shotton where the Wirral – Wrexham line crosses the North Wales main line. The links would facilitate a direct Llandudno – Shrewsbury – Cardiff service.

W4   GOWERTON – PONTARDDULAIS, Swansea.

Reinstatement of a 4 mile line would reduce journey times on the Swansea – Shrewsbury "Heart of Wales" line by avoiding reversals at Llanelli; permit an attractive local service between Ammanford and Swansea and restore Gorseinon to the national rail network.

W5   BRIDGEND – BARRY, Vale of Glamorgan.

A new service is proposed to serve the Vale of Glamorgan and Cardiff International Airport using an existing 19 mile line, which is used for freight and as a diversionary route for passenger trains between Cardiff and Bridgend.   Stations are sought for Llantwit Major, Gileston and St.Athan and at Rhoose/Cardiff Airport

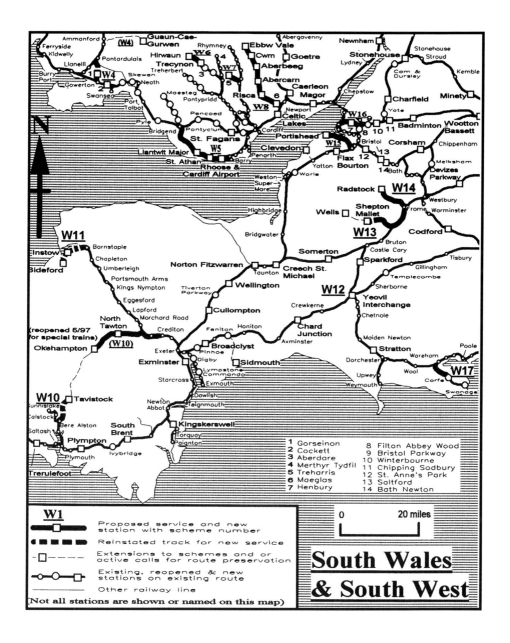

W6 ABERDARE – HIRWAUN, Rhondda Cynon Taff.

A 4 mile extension of the Cardiff – Aberdare service is suggested along the disused freight line as far as Hirwaun to replace the feeder bus link.

W7 TREHARRIS – YSTRAD MYNACH, Caerphilly.

Three new stations at Nelson Llancaiach, Trelewis and Treharris could be served by reopening a freight line and some relaying.

W8 EBBW VALE – NEWPORT, Blaenau Gwent,Caerphilly & Newport

A new service is proposed over the 18 miles of freight railway between Newport and Ebbw Vale, including the possibility of some trains running direct to Cardiff via the Park Junction – Ebbw Junction spur and serving the proposed Celtic Lakes station on the main line. Rail feeder buses would serve Abertillery, the northern suburbs of Ebbw Vale and possibly Tredegar.

Proposed Stations in Wales

County/Station	Line	County/Station	Line
ANGLESEY		**GWYNEDD**	
Amlwch	} Amlwch – Bangor, W1	Caernarfon	Bangor – Caernarfon
Llangefni		Egryn	Barmouth – Harlech
BLAENAU GWENT		**MONMOUTHSHIRE**	
Ebbw Vale	} Ebbw Vale – Newport, W8	Goetre	Newport – Abergavenny
Cwm		**NEWPORT**	
Aberbeeg		Rogerstone	
CAERPHILLY		Bassaleg	} Newport –Ebbw Vale W8
Treharris	} Ystrad Mynach – Treharris W7	Maeglas	
Trelewis		Celtic Lakes	Newport – Cardiff
Nelson Llancaiach		Caerleon	Newport – Abergavenny
Risca		Magor	Newport – Severn Tunnel Jn
Crosskeys			
Abercarn	} Newport –Ebbw Vale W8	**PEMBROKESHIRE**	
Newbridge		Goodwick	Fishguard – Whitland
Crumlin		Templeton	Pembroke – Whitland
Llanhilleth			
CARDIFF		**POWYS**	
Peterston	} Swansea – Cardiff	Buttington	Shrewsbury – Welshpool
St. Fagans		Montgomery	Welshpool – Newtown
CARMARTHENSHIRE		**RHONDDA CYNON TAFF**	
St. Clears	Carmarthen – Whitland	Hirwaun	} Aberdare – Hirwaun, W6
		Trecynon	
DENBIGHSHIRE			
Old Colwyn	Chester – Llandudno	**SWANSEA**	
		Cockett	Swansea – Llanelli
FLINT		Gorseinon	Gowerton –
Queensferry	} Chester – Llandudno		Pontarddulais, W4
Connahs Quay			

70

County/Station	Line	County/Station	Line
Llanharen	Bridgend – Cardiff	**WREXHAM**	
		Gresford	Chester – Wrexham
VALE OF GLAMORGAN		Rossett	
Llantwit Major		Aston	Wrexham – Birkenhead
Gileston & St Athan	Bridgend – Barry W5		
Rhoose & Cardiff		Rhostyllen	
Airport		Rhosllanerchrugog	Wrexham – Shrewsbury
		Cefn Mawr	

SOUTH-WEST ENGLAND

W9   ST. AUSTELL – ST. DENNIS, Cornwall

Restoration of 2 miles of track and use of the 5 mile China Clay traffic line between St. Dennis Junction and Burngullow is proposed for rerouting the Newquay Line trains away from the present route which would also enable the Highways Agency to remove a low rail bridge over the A.30. A beneficial direct Newquay – St. Austell rail service would be secured for both the summer visitors and year round local usage.

W10   TAVISTOCK – BERE ALSTON, Devon

With the feasibility of re-opening this 5.5 mile line being confirmed the County Council is seeking funding approval as this project would help reduce road congestion and develop tourism.   The line originally extended 15 miles northwards to Meldon where the 18 mile Okehampton – Crediton freight line is already the subject of Summer tourist trains to and from Exeter.

W11   BARNSTAPLE – BIDEFORD, Devon

An extension of the Exeter – Barnstaple line along the 9 mile estuary route to Bideford is proposed mostly alongside the Tarka Trail cyclepath.

W12   YEOVIL INTERCHANGE, Somerset.

Given the 2 mile distance between the two Yeovil stations it was once planned to construct a second chord link on the south side.   However the distance and reversals would incur undue time for Bristol – Weymouth trains and the possibility of a new two-level interchange is now being explored.

W13   SHEPTON MALLET – FROME, Somerset

A 2 mile extension of the 7 mile Witham – Cranmore branch to Shepton Mallet is proposed for the resumption of passenger services. A further 5 mile extension along the former trackbed would connect the City of Wells to the rail network benefiting residents and tourists.

W14   RADSTOCK – FROME, Bath and N E Somerset

Restoration of passenger services to Radstock is urged by utilising the 6 mile route beyond the existing 2 mile quarry branch line from Frome.

W15   PORTISHEAD – BRISTOL, Bristol

This 9 mile line is available for freight traffic to Portbury Docks and for a resumption of passenger services.

W16   AVONMOUTH – BRISTOL, Bristol

Use of the 6 mile Filton – Hallen Marsh freight line running across the northern suburbs of Bristol is proposed for a Temple Meads – Avonmouth passenger service with a new station at Cribbs Causeway.

W17   WAREHAM – CORFE, Dorset

The County is lending support to plans by the Swanage Railway to relay 1.5 miles of track and complete a 10.5 mile route for all-year round services.

W18   ANDOVER – LUDGERSHALL, Hampshire/Wiltshire.

The return of passenger services to this 6 mile branch line is sought to serve expanding housing areas.

W19   ROMSEY – EASTLEIGH, Hampshire

The provision of regular passenger services to new stations at Chandlers Ford and Halterworth on the 6 mile Eastleigh – Romsey freight line is sought

W20   FAWLEY – SOUTHAMPTON, Hampshire.

Overcrowded roads and two way traffic between Southampton and the Hythe/Fawley industries justifies new passenger services on the 8.5 mile freight line.

W21   VENTNOR – SHANKLIN, Isle of Wight

A re-opening of the 4 mile route to the original Ventnor terminus is keenly advocated as an important and beneficial extension of the Ryde – Shanklin line.

W22   CAMBERLEY – ALDERSHOT, Surrey/Hampshire.

A Camberley – Frimley Bridge link and a North Camp – Aldershot link would improve passenger access and interchange in the Farnborough area where 4 routes cross, and enable the route via Frimley to be closed. A new Farnborough Cross Interchange Station is proposed.

Proposed stations in South West England

County/Station	Line	County/Station	Line
BATH & N E SOMERSET		**HAMPSHIRE**	
Saltford & Bath Newton	} Bath – Bristol	Frimley Bridge	Blackwater – Farnbough North
Radstock	Radstock – Frome, W14	Chineham	Basingstoke – Reading
		Paulsgrove	
CORNWALL		Wymering	} Portsmouth – Southampton
Carn Brea	Camborne – Redruth	Copnor	
St. Dennis	St. Austell – St. Dennis W9		
Marazion	St Erth – Penzance	Halterworth	} Romsey – Eastleigh, W19
Grampound Road	St Austell – Truro	Chandlers Ford	
Trerulefoot	Saltash – Liskeard	Farnborough Cross	Basingstoke – Woking
		Farlington	Portsmouth – Havant
DEVON		West Totton	
South Brent	} Totnes – Plymouth	Hounsdown	
Plympton		Marchwood	} Southampton – Fawley, W20
Broadclyst	Exeter – Honiton	Hythe	
		Fawley	
Collumpton	Exeter – Tiverton P/W		
Bideford	} Barnstaple – Bideford, W11	**ISLE OF WIGHT**	
Instow		Ventnor	Shanklin-Ventnor,W21
Kingskerwell	Newton Abbot – Torquay	**SOMERSET**	
Tavistock	Bere Alston –Tavistock, W10	Flax Bourton	Bristol – Yatton
		Wellington	Taunton – Tiverton Parkway
North Tawton	Crediton – Okehampton	Shepton Mallet	Frome – Shepton Mallet, W13
DORSET		Creech St Michael	Taunton – Bridgewater
Stratton	Dorchester – Yeovil	Somerton/Langport	Castle Cary – Taunton
Yeovil Interchange	Yeovil Intersection	Sparkford	Castle Cary – Yeovil
		Chard Junction	Crewkerne – Axminster
GLOUCESTERSHIRE			
Churchdown	Gloucester – Cheltenham	**WILTSHIRE**	
Chipping Campden	Evesham – Moreton in Marsh	Corsham	Bath – Chippenham
Charfield	} Gloucester- Bristol	Ludgershall	Andover – Ludgershall, W18
Stonehouse			
Newnham	Gloucester – Lydney	Wootton Bassett	Swindon – Chippenham
		Minety	
SOUTH GLOUCESTERSHIRE		Purton	} Swindon – Gloucester
Winterbourne		Moredon Bridge	
Chipping Sodbury	} Bristol P/W – Swindon	Porton	Salisbury – Andover
Badminton		Devizes Parkway	Westbury – Pewsey
		Wilton	Salisbury – Gillingham

PONTEFRACT TANSHELF, West Yorks. Opened 11.5.92   Photo: Peter Cookson

PRESTWICK AIRPORT, Glasgow.   24.12.96   Photo: Ralph Barker

SOUTH-EAST ENGLAND

E1   CROXLEY LINK, Hertfordshire

With a short mid-way link-up the existing Watford – Croxley branch and the L.U.L. branch from Moor Park & Rickmansworth can provide immediate connection into other urban and longer-distance trains at both ends; rationalise track and train operations; and serve more intermediate locations

E2   ST ALBANS RAIL LINK, Hertfordshire

Provision of a short 1 mile connecting rail link between the two St. Albans stations is an obviously desirable facility benefiting existing and potential rail users.

E3   LUTON – DUNSTABLE, Bedfordshire

Dunstable is the largest town in South East England without a rail link but could be connected by re-opening a disused 5 mile freight line from Luton. The scheme is estimated at about £8m which would include new stations at Luton West and two in Dunstable. Commuters travelling to London and Luton Airport would benefit.

E4   CHINNOR – PRINCES RISBOROUGH, Oxon

As an extension of the Chinnor "heritage" railway Chiltern Railways are considering reopening the line to Aston Rowant where a major Park & Ride facility could be established near Junction 6 for commuters and others to London.

E5   BLETCHLEY – BICESTER/AYLESBURY, Buckinghamshire.

The 20 mile Bletchley – Bicester line forms a key part of the strategic east-west rail route supported by Councils and Consultants for re-opening to Oxford – Bicester – Bletchley – Milton Keynes – Bedford cross-country train services. An 11 mile southern link from Claydon Junction to Aylesbury now used for freight trains is also a candidate for trains extended to Milton Keynes.

E6   BEDFORD – SANDY, Bedfordshire

Re-opening of this 8.5 mile portion of the former Oxford – Cambridge cross-country route was a clear recommendation by Steer, Davies and Gleave to form a strategic freight and passenger route linking East Anglia with several radial main lines. Plans for new roads in Bedford will frustrate protection and re-opening of the railway.

E7   KETTERING – CORBY, Northamptonshire.

Although an earlier Corby rail shuttle was withdrawn due to unreliable and irregular trains, there continues to be an outstanding need for this sizeable town to secure a good rail service. A through diesel train service linking Bletchley – Bedford – Kettering – Corby is one possibility. Also a direct and fast Bedford – Corby – Peterborough service could be achieved with reinstatement of a 3 mile chord link between Seaton and South Luffenham.

E8   CAMBRIDGE – ST. IVES, Cambridgeshire

The County Council are supporting this 11 mile rail scheme costing £20m rather than a busway. 400 people attended a meeting in St. Ives to support re-opening for an estimated 3,500 users per day. The scheme has potential to link with other stations in the Cambridge area, especially Addenbrookes south of the city. Rail privatisation has seen both start-up and running costs increased.

E9   MARCH – WISBECH, Cambridgeshire

Resumption of passenger services is sought for this 7.5 mile freight line linking Wisbech in the Fens to the Peterborough – March – Ely line.

E10   WYMONDHAM – DEREHAM, Norfolk

This 11.5 mile single line could be re-opened to tourists and local passengers and provide a useful Dereham- Norwich service.

E11   BRAINTREE – STANSTED – BISHOPS STORTFORD, Essex.

A new 14 mile route linking-up the Braintree and Stansted branches is proposed.

E12   WITHAM – MALDON, Essex

Restoration of the 6 mile Maldon branch is being sought to serve this popular coastal town

E13   CHANNEL TUNNEL RAIL LINK, London/Essex/Kent

The much debated and well overdue 68 mile high-speed rail link between London and the Channel Tunnel could become a reality in 2010. A Government contribution of £1.4 billion is being made to the £3 billion cost. In London, a new international station is proposed at St. Pancras by increasing the number of platforms and doubling the length of the station. Eurostar trains to and from North of London will be able to by-pass St. Pancras. Through east London the line will be in tunnel for almost 20 Km, emerging for a new interchange station at Stratford.

The line will go under the Thames in twin-bore tunnels and emerge at a new Ebbsfleet station in North Kent which will be an M25 parkway for both domestic and international passengers. The expansion of Ashford into an international station was completed in early 1996 and the C.T.R.L. will carry Eurostar services, international freight, as well as Kent commuter trains

E14   WOOLWICH RAIL TUNNEL, London

A one mile rail tunnel linking Silvertown and Woolwich Arsenal is proposed to open-up many new and faster journey opportunities between north and south London in the east. It would relieve the overcrowded London Bridge services; the congested Blackwall Tunnel; facilitate development of Thamesmead, Silvertown and the Royal Docks and, via the Canning Town Jubilee Line Interchange, North Greenwich, Canary Wharf, Canada Water and Bermondsey and improve access to London City Airport

E15   EAST LONDON EXTENSION, London

Utilising the East London rail tunnel under the River Thames between Wapping and Rotherhithe this new rail link could connect-up Dalston Kingsland on the North London Line using the former Broad Street route to the present Whitechapel – Wapping – Canada Water – Surrey Quays line and via a restored link to Peckham to   provide through services to Dulwich and many destinations south of Tulse Hill

E16   NORTH – SOUTH CROSSRAIL,   London.

A new link between Kings Cross and Victoria via Piccadilly Circus has been proposed by the Central London Rail Study either as a mainline gauge cross-town link or as a LUL Chelsea – Hackney Tube

E17   EAST – WEST CROSSRAIL , London

The construction of a 7 mile twin tunnel B.R. East-West Crossrail was approved for a 1997 start but has been put on hold. Between Royal Oak and Bethnal Green the tunnel route is likely to have 5 stations and the overall cost is some £2.0bn. The tunnel journey time will be 11 minutes.

E18   WATERLOO – LIVERPOOL ST, London.

Utilising an enlarged and extended Waterloo & City line a third cross-rail facility can be secured offering a multitude of connections; greater utilisation of stock and much better access to the City via Liverpool St – Blackfriars – Waterloo. The scheme would supplement the East-West cross-rail project.

E19   HEATHROW – PADDINGTON/ST.PANCRAS   London

Work started on this £300m project in late 1993 and this 16 mile route is due to be completed in mid-1998. The new Class 332 emu's will make the 16 minute journey every 15 minutes, 18 hours a day. British Airports Authority, who now own the new rail facility, will also operate a Heathrow – St. Pancras train service every 15 minutes via the Acton – Neasden – Cricklewood route which is to be electrified. Trains will call at West Hampstead, Ealing and Hayes from 1998 taking 35 minutes to complete the journey

E20   HEATHROW – FELTHAM,   London

Several London Boroughs have promoted a complimentary rail link to Heathrow from Feltham on the Waterloo – Staines line. There are also proposals to site two "gateway" stations to the north and south of the Airport at Stockley Park on the Great Western line and at Feltham

E21   HEATHROW WESTERN CONNECTION

A study is underway into the scope for new rail links to the west enabling Terminal 5 to be served by trains from the West Country , Wales and the Midlands

E22   GUILDFORD – CRANLEIGH,   Surrey

This line closed in 1965, just as Cranleigh was on the brink of major expansion. Both Surrey County Council and Railtrack have investigated re-opening and agree that it was possible. It would help to take traffic from the congested A281 and bring the only significant town in Surrey not rail connected back onto the map.

E23   EPSOM – CHESSINGTON,   Surrey

A new 3 mile rail link to connect Chessington with Epsom is proposed to serve housing estates, Adventure World and Hospitals.

E24   REDHILL FLYOVER,   Surrey

A new flyover is urged as an essential direct east – west link for freight trains avoiding London on the Ashford – Tonbridge – Guildford – Reading route. The facility would avoid time consuming reversals and conflicts with the intensive passenger services at Redhill Station

E25   LEWES – UCKFIELD – TUNBRIDGE WELLS,   East Sussex

Restoration of the 8 mile Uckfield – Lewes line has been a long-standing campaign that has gained the support of local authorities and the former Network SouthEast. A Mott MacDonald study in 1996 confirmed that re-opening of both Uckfield – Lewes and a single track Groombridge – Tunbridge Wells Central line is physically possible and strongly recommended as a through route.

Proposed Stations in the South-East

County/Station	Line	County/Station	Line
BEDFORDSHIRE		**ESSEX**	
Oakley Sharnbrook	} Wellingborough – Bedford	Clacton North	Clacton – Colchester
		Maldon	New branch, E12
Luton West Dunstable North Dunstable East	} Luton – Dunstable New service, E3	Ardleigh Hawkwell	Colchester – Ipswich Southend – Billericay
BERKSHIRE		Springfield Stanway	} Colchester – Chelmsford
Southcote	Reading – Pewsey		
Woodley	Reading – Twyford	Canvey Parkway West Laindon	} Southend – Upminster
BUCKINGHAMSHIRE			
Bedgrove	Aylesbury – Amersham	**KENT**	
Loudwater	Beaconsfield – High Wycombe	Chart Leacon Five Oaks Green	} Tonbridge – Ashford
Winslow Claydon Junction Quainton Road	} Bletchley – Aylesbury, E5	Twydall Pegwell Bay Welling Corner	Rainham – Gillingham Dover – Ramsgate Dartford – Eltham
South Aylesbury West Wycombe	} Aylesbury – High Wycombe	Ebbsfleet	C.T.R.L. E13
Castlethorpe	Wolverton – Northampton	Kings North Dartford Parkway	Ashford – Hastings Dartford – Gravesend
CAMBRIDGESHIRE		**LONDON**	
Coldhams lane Waterfenton Little Thetford Nth Cambridge Parkway	} Cambridge – Ely	Walworth Camberwell	} Blackfriars – Herne Hill
		Eastfields	Streatham – Mitcham
Cherry Hinton Fulbourn Six Mile Bottom	} Cambridge – Newmarket	Western Gateway Stratford Market	} Stratford – North Woolwich
Prickwillow	Ely – Norwich	Brixton HL Bermondsey	} South London Line London Bridge –
Soham	Ely – Bury St. Edmunds		Denmark Hill – Victoria
Little Shelford Addenbrooke's Hospital	} Cambridge – Royston	White City Shepherds Bush Earls Court Chelsea Harbour	} Clapham – Willesden
Offord and Buckden	St.Neots – Huntingdon		
Werrington Deeping St. James	} Peterborough – Spalding	Hagerston Hoxton Bishopsgate	} Dalston – East London, E15.
Sth Peterborough Newtown	Peterborough – Huntingdon	Lea Bridge Picketts Lock	} Stratford – Cheshunt
St. Ives Swavesey Longstanton Oakington Histon Kings Hedges	} Cambridge – St.Ives, E8	Stratford Int'l	C T R L, E13
		NORFOLK	
		Dereham	Wymondham – Dereham, E10
Wisbech	March – Wisbech, E9	Forncett	Norwich – Ipswich
EAST SUSSEX		Cringleford Towse	} Norwich – Thetford
Glyne Gap Stone Cross	} Eastbourne – Hastings		

County/Station	Line	County/Station	Line
NORTHAMPTONSHIRE		Bealings	Ipswich – Lowestoft
Roade	Northampton – Wolverton	Great Cornard	Sudbury – Colchester
Corby	Kettering – Corby	Norwich Rd, Ipswich Warren Heath Felixstowe Maritime }	Ipswich – Felixstowe
Desborough Irchester Burton Latimer }	Market Harborough – Bedford	**SURREY**	
		Epsom Wells	Epsom – Leatherhead
OXFORDSHIRE		Fetcham Merrow & Burpham }	Guildford – Leatherhead
Shrivenham Wantage Kidlington }	Didcot – Swindon Oxford – Banbury	Park Barn Stoughton	Guildford – Aldershot Guildford – Woking
SUFFOLK		Bramley Cranleigh }	Guildford – Cranleigh, E22
Bentley	Ipswich – Colchester	Adventure World	Epsom – Chessington, E23
Mellis Finningham Bramford Claydon }	Norwich – Ipswich	**WEST SUSSEX**	
		Tinsley Green	Gatwick – Three Bridges

SMETHWICK GALTON BRIDGE, West Midlands. Jan 1997   Photo: Alan Bevan

Chapter 6
NEW RAILWAYS AND RE-OPENINGS AROUND EUROPE

It is illuminating to look at the experience of other European countries, particularly those with a geography, economy and lifestyle similar to our own.

Most West European countries saw some rail closures in the 1950s and 1960s, though not usually on anything like the same scale as the Beeching era cuts in Great Britain. Since then, the growth of road traffic and its associated environmental effects have caused many governments to look again at the rail alternative. Some countries, notably France, have reintroduced tramways or light rapid transit in their cities; others, particularly the former West Germany, invested large sums in new underground systems, often integrating these with existing tram networks. In this chapter we concentrate on the ways in which different European states have developed heavy conventional rail.

FRANCE

The French have built new railways on a grand scale. This is most obvious to the Eurostar passenger who travels from London to the Channel Tunnel at a relatively modest speed on lines built in the 19th century and electrified in the 1950s and 1960s. Once through the Tunnel, the Eurostar accelerates dramatically and the chef de train is soon announcing a maximum speed of 300 kph (186 mph). The journey to Paris is almost entirely via the 330 kilometre long Ligne à Grande Vitesse (High Speed Line) built in the early 1990s. It was in the mid 1970s that the concept of new High Speed lines was conceived, together with the Train à Grande Vitesse (High Speed Train) to run on them. The first such route was opened in stages from Paris to Lyon in 1981 and 1983. It led to a dramatic reduction in internal airline travel between the two cities and stabilised the growth in motorway traffic. During the mid 1980s, traffic on the A6 motorway between Paris and the South East remained constant and, even since then, it has grown at a much slower pace than on the motorways to Metz and Caen, where there is no competition from High Speed Rail. Two other High Speed Lines were then built – the Atlantique from Paris to destinations in Brittany and the South West (opened in 1989); and the Nord to Lille, Calais and the Belgian border (opened in 1993). A junction line has also been constructed around the eastern outskirts of Paris to link all three radial routes. Plans for an eastern route to Strasbourg and the German border are currently beset with financial difficulties. The High Speed Lines have very few intermediate stations. These have been built at a small number of towns such as Macon and Vendôme, aimed particularly at the "park and ride" market, and a somewhat controversial Gare Haute Picardie was built in the open countryside to the east of Amiens. Critics of the "park and ride" station on the LGV Nord referred to it as the "gare des betteraves" (Beetroot Station).

The Fédération Nationale des Associations d'Usagers des Transports (FNAUT), the voluntary body representing French public transport passengers, published an in-depth article in November 1996 on the future of the TGV. While stressing support in principle for the new lines and their modest extension, FNAUT made a number of constructive criticisms:-

1. Compulsory reservations and high fares are a deterrent to some passengers
2. Services have been allowed to deteriorate on some parallel classic routes, such as Paris – Dijon.
3 The potential of the TGVs for transporting high value goods could be exploited much more. For example, only one TGV route, the South East, carried postal traffic.
4. The High Speed Trains need to be much better integrated into the rest of the network. This only happens to a limited extent with, for example, a couple of TGVs-Nord starting their journeys on the classic network at Boulogne-Ville. FNAUT suggest that tilting trains could be a more effective way of increasing speeds on some classic routes feeding into the TGV network.

In and around Paris, cross-city lines have been built to form the RER (Reseau Express Regional – Regional Express Network). These are comparable to the east-west Crossrail proposed between Liverpool Street and Paddington in London, in that they can be used by suburban trains from the main line network. The number of stations is relatively small but there is full integration with the Metro or Underground. Four RER lines exist already and two others are planned or are under construction.

New or re-opened stations or halts on existing lines are encountered less often than in our country. Sometimes these have been built to serve new estates or entertainment complexes, such as Walibi-Schtroumpf serving a leisure park on the site of an old steelworks near Metz to serve walkers and cyclists. In other cases, such as Fontainebleau-Foret in the forest of that name near Paris to serve walkers and cyclists. Other new stations include Le Banlay near Nevers; Le Pardieu near Clermont Ferrand and Kerlann near Rennes. In Provence, the route from Nice to Digne has re-opened and from time to time there have been proposals to re-open the cross-border line between Canfranc and Oloron in the Pyrenees, originally closed because of flood damage.

GERMANY

In the years before reunification in 1990, the two German states tended to concentrate their rail development on North-South links. As early as 1963, the Vogelfluglinie ("Beeline" or literally "Bird's Flight Line") was built linking Puttgarden, on the Baltic island of Fehmarn, to the mainland and creating a faster train and ferry link between Copenhagen, Hamburg and points south. In the 1980s, "Neubaustrecken" comparable to the French high speed lines, were built from Hannover to Würzburg and from Mannheim to Stuttgart. These are used by Inter City Express (ICE) trains and closely integrated into the rest of the network. The Hannover – Würzburg line includes a considerable amount of tunnelling and a brand new station at Kassel Wilhelmshöhe, where there is easy interchange with local and regional services. A "Neubaustrecke" from Frankfurt to Cologne is due to open in 2000 and a further stretch is planned through the hills of the Thüringer Wald from Erfurt southwards into Bavaria.

Reunification is restoring Berlin to its former importance as the country's capital and has led to a shift of investment into East-West links during the 1990s. Local railway management took their own initiative in restoring passenger services across the former border between Walkenried and Nordhausen, on the southern side of the Harz mountains, for example. On the northern side, a new link between Vienenburg and Stapelburg was opened in 1996, enabling trains to run direct from the Hannover area to Halle, Leipzig and other destinations in Saxony. Work is also well advanced on reinstating the former main line from Salzwedel to Uelzen, to provide a more direct route from Saxony to Hamburg and from Berlin to Bremen. High speed routes are being created from Hannover to Berlin by building new running lines alongside existing track via Wolfsburg and Brandenburg. These are "Ausbaustrecken" (upgraded routes) rather than "Neubaustrecken " (newly built routes).

The main line from Berlin to Hamburg has been electrified, with some realignment, but there are also plans for a Maglev monorail system between the two cities called "Transrapid", it has been promoted by the Government and some private companies partly because of its export potential. Critics of the latter, however, have suggested that the demand would in no way justify the expense and, of course, it could not be integrated into the rest of the network. They have also pointed out that the Maglev idea originated at a time when it was not thought possible for conventional railways to carry trains at more than 200 kph. In and around Berlin itself, certain of the links that were severed during the city's four decades of division have been restored and others are planned. So far, S-bahn (electric suburban train) links from Wannsee to Potsdam, Westkreuz to Schönefeld airport and Jungfernheide to Ostkreuz have been re-opened and it is planned to restore the direct link from Henningsdorf to the city centre. A new North – South tunnel is to be constructed for use by main line trains.

Frankfurt now has an East – West tunnel, rather like the Crossrail proposed for London, and a similar cross-city link is planned for Stuttgart. In the 1970s a link was built to enable main line trains to serve Frankfurt Airport while the airport at Düsseldorf has also been provided with a rail spur. Its terminus could become a through station served by all Inter City trains if current plans to re-direct the Düsseldorf – Duisburg main line go ahead. The re-opening of some rural lines is also on the agenda in certain regions of Germany. In Schleswig – Holstein in the far north, for example, a plan was published in October 1996 to develop seven "Regional-Express" routes to complement the Inter City lines. This will involve re-opening six lines closed between 1953 and 1984 and increasing the network from 1306 km to 1416 km, together with 27 new or re-opened stations.

NETHERLANDS

In the early 1990s, the Dutch Government adopted policies deliberately aimed at increasing the market share of public transport. These included planning strategies in which the actual or potential availability of public transport would help decide where development would take place. In the "Randstad" – the highly urbanised circle that encompasses Amsterdam, The Hague, Rotterdam and Utrecht – millions of guilders have been invested in the rail infrastructure, with track widening, new junctions and new stations, including six betwen Amsterdam and Utrecht. One concern has been to relieve bottlenecks and it was partly for this reason that the Maas Tunnel was opened on the line between Rotterdam and Dordrecht in 1994. to replace an earlier bridge and viaduct.

Completely new lines have also been built, for a variety of reasons. In the 1970s, the Zoetermeer Line was opened on the eastern fringes of The Hague, with electric suburban trains describing two circles as they serve closely spaced stations in a new town. In the early 1980s a new line was built from Leiden to Amsterdam serving Schiphol Airport and used by international as well as domestic trains. The reclamation of Flevoland from the southern part of the Ijsselmeer (formerly Zuyder Zee) led to the construction of a new railway across the new land. In 1986 the Flevo Line was opened from Weesp to the new town of Lelystad, serving a further growing town, Almere, on the way. In the extreme south of the country the freight line from Heerlen across the German border to Herzogenrath was re-opened to passengers and the Maastricht – Aachen service diverted over it. However this also caused the line from Schin-op-Geul to Aachen to be closed and the village of Simpelveld losing its service. A preservation society is now reported to have taken over this line. Plans are being developed for a new freight line through the Betuwe region from Dordrecht to the German border near Arnhem. The separation of the infrastructure from operations, and the creation of "Railned", a Dutch equivalent of Railtrack, has led to some innovations, by "Lovers Rail", a private train operator. In 1996 the "Kennemerstrand Express" was run from Amsterdam, partly over freight-only track to the coast and this was extended in the summer of 1997 to Ijmuiderstrand and the Scandinavian Seaways ferry terminal. "Lovers Rail" also propose a service from Amsterdam to the re-opened station at Lise, between Haarlem and Leiden, during the tulip season.

BELGIUM

The major new railway project in Belgium at present is the high speed line from Lille to Brussels, which will be used by Eurostar services from London and by high-speed tri-voltage Thalys trains from Paris to Brussels, Amsterdam and Cologne. It is being constructed by a special company, TUC Rail, in which the SNCB (the Belgian national railway) holds 75% of the shares and the first section, from Lille to Antoing, was brought into use in June 1996, reducing the Paris – Brussels journey time by 30 minutes.

High speed routes are also planned from Brussels to Antwerp(where the central terminus would be converted to a through station) and on across the Dutch border; and from Brussels to Liege and Aachen, across the German border. These projects will be achieved partly by upgrading existing routes for 160 kph or 200 kph running, and partly by building three more stretches of new line for 300 kph running. When the construction programme is complete Belgium will have some 209 km of new rail route – this in a small country whose national rail network currently totals 3,400 route kilometres.

Brussels was one of the first capital cities in more recent times to link its termini with a cross-city tunnel, when the 6-track main line under the city centre was completed in 1952. Brussels Airport was linked to the main line network and Schumann station was built in the late 1960s to serve the then EEC headquarters. The 1980s saw the re-opening to passengers of short branches to Genk and Eupen, the largest town of the German-speaking minority in eastern Belgium. The latter was provided with a brand new station and through trains to Spa and to Brussels and Ostend. New construction also took place at the other end of the country when the Knokke branch interfered with the expansion of Zeebrugge harbour! A diversion was built so that trains from Bruges to Knokke now avoid Zeebrugge and the latter's former through station has become a terminus.

LUXEMBOURG

A new station has been built at Howald and Luxembourg railways trains now continue across the border south of Esch-sur-Alzette on a formerly freight-only line to serve Audun-la-Tiche in France.

ITALY AND THE ALPINE COUNTRIES

Direttissima lines are being built north and south of Rome and a cross-city tunnel has been opened in Milan. A cross-border link has been opened from Breil-sur-Roya to Ventimiglia. In the "foot" of Italy a new line and tunnel has been built to link Paola and Cosenza, replacing a former rack railway. Ambitious plans have been drawn up for three "base tunnels" through the Alps between Italy and Switzerland or Austria. These would be longer, and at a lower level, than existing tunnels thus reducing the gradients and curves which present-day trains have to negotiate.

In 1994 the Swiss voted in a referendum to ban transit freight from the country's roads by 2004. This decision gave added impetus to the plans for base tunnels and work has now started on the Gotthard Base Tunnel. A total of 125 km of new railway is to be completed by 2005, including new approach lines and a tunnel which, at 57 km, will be the longest in the world. The Lotschberg BaseTunnel, on which work has not yet started, would be Y-shaped, with an underground junction and a total length of 41.9 km. The third scheme is the 65-km Brenner Base Tunnel which would benefit traffic from Germany and Austria to Italy. Funding is still being discussed in the three countries, but the 15 km Innsbruck avoiding line, completed in 1994, would be an integral part of the project.

Meanwhile a 9.5 km avoiding line for Grauholz in Switzerland was opened in May 1995 and is intended to link with a 54-km new line between Olten and Bern. The go-ahead has also been given for a new line between Mutenz and Liestal. In Austria work is in progress between Vienna and St Polten as part of an upgrading of the main line to Salzburg and on a 12-km base tunnel from the capital to Graz on the Semmering Pass route. These Austrian and Swiss schemes will not only reduce the travelling times between the major cities but will also benefit international passenger and freight trains.

DENMARK

Much of Denmark consists of islands and so its transport infrastructure problems are not totally unlike those of the United Kingdom. A further interesting link is that British engineers, including William Radford and Peto, Brassey and Betts, were involved in the building of some of the earliest Danish railways.

Denmark's answer to the Channel tunnel, the Great Belt Link, was opened on June 1st 1997. This 25.0 kilometre link from Nyborg to Korsor involves an 8 km tunnel from Zealand to the tiny island of Sprogo and a 6.6 km bridge from there to Funen. It reduces by an hour the travelling times from Copenhagen to the

Jutland peninsula and the rest of Continental Europe, and is used by international trains such as Paris – Copenhagen. Construction of the link has also enabled the Danish Post Office to switch more of its traffic from road and air to rail.

The next major project will be a fixed link across the Sound linking the Danish Railways to those of Sweden. There will be a rail link from Copenhagen to Kastrup Airport, on the island of Amager, just south of the city. Work started in 1994 and by the winter of 1998 it is planned to have this line in use. The new railway will continue under the Sound by a 3.8-km tunnel rising to an artificial island to be called Peberholm. A 7-km bridge will link Peberholm to Lernacken, south of the Swedish city of Malmo and the project is due to be completed in the year 2000. A north-south tunnel under Malmo has also been authorised by the Swedish Government but is not due for completion until 2007. Both the South Link and the Great Belt Link include a motorway as well as a railway.

On a more modest note, but in its way just as significant, a considerable number of new stations have been built on existing lines in Denmark, principally on the 13 private railways, particularly following a new Act governing these which was passed by the Danish Parliament in 1984. The private railways are, in fact, owned by local authorities and provide feeder services into the national DSB system. Since 1985, seven new halts have been opened by private lines on the Jutland peninsula, sometimes to serve new suburbs or leisure centres. At least four new stations have been opened on Zealand, one on Funen and four on Jutland on the main DSB network. Sometimes these are to serve hospitals (as at Odense and Vejle), school complexes (at Naestved) or a university (at Roskilde). Hinnerup station, north of Arhus, was re-opened in 1994 and is served by local and some Inter City trains.

Rail development on Jutland has also included a new spur from Taulov to the Little Belt Bridge, south of Fredericia, in 1993, enabling freight trains to avoid reversal at this busy junction; and electrification of the main line down the east coast to the German border. When the Sound link is complete, electric trains will be able to operate all the way from Narvik, north of the Arctic circle, via the Swedish iron ore fields, down to the Mediterranean. Finally, mention should be made of the west coast of Jutland, where re-opening of the 17-km cross-border link between Tonder and Niebüll is being considered.

IRELAND

The most dramatic rail development in Ireland has taken place in Belfast. Like many cities on the British mainland, it suffered from having radial routes built by different private companies and run quite separately from each other. There were three termini, Great Victoria Street, York Road and Queens Quay, serving the routes to Dublin, Larne and Bangor respectively, and a cross-city Belfast central railway linking the Dublin and Bangor routes had fallen into disuse. An attempt to integrate Londonderry services better into the rest of the network was made in the 1980s when the freight-only line from Lisburn to Antrim was re-opened to passengers together with four stations on it. However, this in turn led to greater isolation for the Larne route.

The first stage of redrawing the rail map of Belfast came when the Belfast Central Railway was rebuilt and new stations built at Belfast Central and Botanic. This led to the closure of Great Victoria Street, however. Then in 1994, a completely new 2-km route was constructed from the Larne line, with a new Yorkgate through station adjacent to the former York Road terminus, enabling trains from Larne to reach central Belfast and continue southwards. Finally, a new Great Victoria Street terminus and triangular junction have been built, particularly for commuter traffic. Funding by the European Regional Development fund enabled the last two of these projects to go ahead. A few stations on Northern Ireland Railways have also been re-opened or newly built, notably Newry, Poyntzpass, Dhu Varren, Culleybackey, Scarva and Bellarena; while a new station was provided for the University at Coleraine.

In the south, the most significant re-openings are of commuter stations between Dublin and Maynooth on the line to Sligo. At one point, all stations between Dublin and Mullingar has been closed. The other main line westwards out of the city, from Heuston to Kildare, has also seen suburban stations re-opened. Other station re-openings on Iarnrod Eireann include Kilcoole, Foxford and Ennis. The regeneration of Dublin suburban traffic is completed by DART, the electrification of the cross-city route from Bray on the Rosslare line to Howth. The growth in business on this service has so far led to two new stations being built. Modest new construction has also taken place at Lavinstown in County Kilkenny, where a new triangular junction enables freight trains to and from the port of Waterford to proceed without having to reverse at Kilkenny. As in the North, money from the European Regional Development Fund has contributed significantly towards rail improvements in the Republic.

WHIFFLET, Nr Motherwell.   23.12.96   Photo: Ralph Barker

YARM, Tees-side. Opening day 20.2.96   Photo: Reg' Rlys North East

Railway Development Society

Many of the stations opened or proposed in this book have been the subject of ideas and promotion by the voluntary Railway Development Society. It is an independent organisation with Branches throughout Great Britain. We campaign for the development of our rail network for both freight and passenger services as an essential part of a sustainable environment.

Why not join us? All members receive regular News magazines covering National & Branch affairs. We publish many interesting booklets, organise conferences, hold meetings and other activities for members. Standard membership is just £15 p.a. with concessions for students and senior citizens. Write now for details to R.D.S., 13 Arnhill Road, Gretton, Corby, Northants, NN17 3DN.

In addition to its quarterly journal 'Railwatch' the R.D.S. published books and reports on the current rail scene and important campaign issues. For an up-to-date catalogue listing over 50 items please write to RDS Sales. Broadheath, Fishers Hill, Catisfield, Fareham, Hants, PO15 5QY.

Acknowledgements

The Railway Development Society is grateful to its many members throughout Great Britain who have contributed information, photographs, and maps for this book. The assistance of Ralph Barker, Peter Clark, Alan Crowhurst, Gerard Duddridge, Erland Egefors, Trevor Garrod and Andrew Macfarlane is particularly appreciated.